SIX SIGMA IN HR
TRANSFORMATION

Orion Partners

Orion Partners are leading independent advisers in HR Transformation. Established in 2002, we have led and managed HR Transformation programmes for over thirty blue chip clients and our client base covers leading organisations in both private and public sectors.

We help organisations to succeed in their HR transformation by enabling them to:

- Clarify and define HR's strategy and role relative to the business.
- Decide on the most suitable operating model for HR, including the option of shared services or outsourcing.
- Select and implement the right technology solutions.
- Assess and select the right people.
- Develop the skills and mindset to succeed.
- Make the transformation happen on the ground.

Our unique focus is the whole range of HR transformation activities. We pride ourselves on the independence and practical nature of our advice and our focus on identifying and capturing the benefits in our design and implementation. We have skills and expertise in scoping, design and change management of the transition.

We have a have a broad base of functional, industry and global experience. Together with deep knowledge of HR and what makes it work successfully. We undertake regular research in the HR field including our unique studies on the difference that makes a difference in HR Business partners and HR Leaders

If you would like to find out more, please visit www.orion-partners. com or call us on +44 (0) 207 993 4699

Six Sigma in HR Transformation

Achieving Excellence in Service Delivery

Mircea Albeanu and *Ian Hunter*
with *Jo Radford*

Routledge
Taylor & Francis Group

LONDON AND NEW YORK

First published 2010 by Gower Publishing

Published 2016 by Routledge
2 Park Square, Milton Park, Abingdon, Oxon OX14 4RN
711 Third Avenue, New York, NY 10017, USA

Routledge is an imprint of the Taylor & Francis Group, an informa business

British Library Cataloguing in Publication Data
Albeanu, Mircea.
  Six Sigma in HR transformation : achieving excellence in
  service delivery. -- (The Gower HR transformation series)
  1. Six sigma (Quality control standard) 2. Service
  industries--Quality control. 3. Consumer satisfaction--
  Statistical methods.
  I. Title II. Series III. Hunter, Ian, 1963–
  658.5'62-dc22

Library of Congress Control Number: 2010927580

ISBN 13: 978-0-566-09164-3 (pbk)

Contents

List of Figures

List of Tables

# **(1) Introduction**

'Six Sigma *is the most important initiative we have ever undertaken.'*

Jack Welch, then CEO – General Electric

In the business world, especially in manufacturing or quality management, the term *Six Sigma* usually refers to a set of tools and methodologies developed by Motorola to improve processes by eliminating defects.

But why should the HR professional care what *Six Sigma* is or how it can be applied in the HR function? In Orion Partners' experience there are ten key reasons why HR professionals should be interested:

1. **Create excellence in process delivery** – To deliver the day-to-day service consistently and focus more on strategic goals, HR must make sure that its processes run smoothly with no or minimal problems. *Six Sigma* is an excellent way of delivering process excellence.

2. **Reduce defects** – From queries that are time consuming to resolve to wrong salaries or inaccurate employee data, all HR processes are prone to producing multiple

defects during delivery. Sometimes these defects remain unnoticed until they start to cause problems and when this happens they can affect the organisation at a much higher level, significantly impacting areas such as finance, customer satisfaction or even the legality of the business. It is therefore a high priority to detect and minimise the number of defects produced. Achieving the *Six Sigma* level or 99.9997 per cent flawless transactions, may not be possible in all HR processes, but by taking the *Six Sigma* approach defects can often be reduced substantially.

3. **Reduce scrap/increase efficiency** – Through lean techniques, combined with *Six Sigma* methodologies and tools, HR can work to reduce resources lost in ineffective, sometimes unnecessary tasks and still deliver the service within the required standards.

4. **Create a quality focused mindset** – For HR to deliver value, the whole function must be focused on quality, as measured via service level agreements (SLAs) or customer satisfaction metrics. The *Six Sigma* philosophy introduces this kind of mindset and, in organisation-wide implementations, even embeds it into the culture of the organisation.

5. **Benefit from best practice** – For HR to undertake effective reviews of processes that will deliver maximum benefit, *Six Sigma* offers best practice tools and techniques which have been proven in many organisations.

6. **Bring clarity to the processes** – Processes can contain hidden problems that sooner or later affect the service being delivered, such as bottlenecks, unduly long

processing time, or a significant number of defects. Two of the main phases of *Six Sigma* improvement projects focus specifically on bringing clarity to the process and its metrics, using statistical tools that can offer deep insight into the inner workings of the process, as well as the external factors affecting it, enabling the delivery of improvements.

7. **Use a structured scientific approach** – *Six Sigma* is, of course, not the only option for product or service improvement. However it is a proven method based on well-structured scientific methodologies that provides a framework to be applied in any process improvement project.

8. **Speak the same language** – Time may be lost due to communication issues that arise from use of terminology or jargon. *Six Sigma* offers a consistent language that reduces confusion in delivering improvements.

9. **Maintain control of your processes** – It is a common problem that an efficiently designed process can quickly develop issues and revert to inefficiency. One of the tasks of *Six Sigma* is to make sure that after delivery, the new or improved process will continue to produce consistent results for as long as the process functions.

10. **Strengthen your business case** – Given the proven track record that *Six Sigma* has in both the service and production industry, with some of the world's largest organisations benefiting from its results, HR's business case to improve itself can gain more credibility if based on *Six Sigma*; especially where the methodology is already used in other parts of the business.

A note for our readers: We have written this book to give HR teams an insight into the value *Six Sigma* can add to the transformation process. It is not intended to be a replacement for standard *Six Sigma* texts which give detailed explanations of the tools and formulae used in the *Six Sigma* process. Instead our intention is to shed light on when and how these tools may be useful to an HR team.

THE EVOLUTION OF *SIX SIGMA*

The main concepts that *Six Sigma* uses date back to the eighteenth century and were created by people who found ways to describe chaos, randomness or astronomical phenomena, through mathematical equations such as Pierre Laplace, Abraham de Moivre and Carl Friedrich Gauss. It took over 200 years for these concepts to be applied in the business world for improving quality in both manufacturing and services.

The cornerstone of *Six Sigma* is the normal probability distribution, also known as a bell curve (named due to its resemblance to a bell). This distribution was introduced by Abraham de Moivre in an article published in 1733 and then in the second edition of his book, *The Doctrine of Chances*, in 1738.

Its significance comes from the fact that the distributions of many natural phenomena are approximately normally distributed, meaning that the chart of their frequency of occurrence resembles the bell curve.

Figure 1.1 opposite shows the sigma levels plotted on the normal distribution.

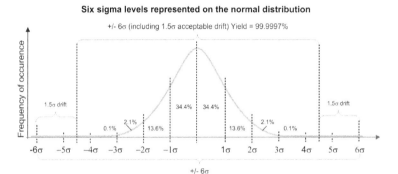

Figure 1.1 is captioned below.

Six sigma levels represented on the normal distribution

+/- 6σ (including 1.5σ acceptable drift) Yield = 99.9997%

Frequency of occurrence

1.5σ drift

34.4% 34.4%

1.5σ drift

0.1% 2.1% 13.6% 13.6% 2.1% 0.1%

-6σ -5σ -4σ -3σ -2σ -1σ 1σ 2σ 3σ 4σ 5σ 6σ

+/- 6σ

Figure 1.1   *Six Sigma* levels represented on the normal distribution

Observation in many industries has shown that the recorded data, such as dimensions of parts (in manufacturing) or cost per transaction (in services), often fits the bell curve pattern, which enables analysts to perform various statistical analyses on the data.

A STATISTICAL METRIC

In statistical terms, sigma represents the standard deviation; a measure of the variability within a population around the mean. For example, the mean height in a population may be five foot nine inches, with the majority of people, say 68 per cent, having a height which is within three inches of that mean. This represents one standard deviation from the mean. The next deviation, the second, covers all people with a height within six inches of the mean, approximately 95 per cent of the population. *Six Sigma* represents the population that falls within +/- six standard deviations from the mean. If you apply *Six Sigma* to a payroll process for instance, and are calculating the acceptable number of defects allowable per million payroll calculations, then to fall within *Six Sigma* parameters, there would only be 3.4 defects per million allowed. See table below.

Sigma Level	Defects per million opportunities
1 Sigma	690,000
2 Sigma	308,000
3 Sigma	66,800
4 Sigma	6,210
5 Sigma	230
Six Sigma	3.4

This means, for example, that a payroll process operating at a *Six Sigma* level will have less than 3.4 errors per million opportunities.

A QUALITY MANAGEMENT METRIC

Six Sigma as a quality improvement methodology appeared in the 1970s after a Japanese firm took over one of Motorola's TV factories in the United States. It was not long before they were producing the same televisions in the same factory at the same or even lower costs, but with 95 per cent less defects. This significant improvement in performance levels sent a clear message to Motorola; in order to survive it needed to rethink its approach to quality. Bob Galvin, the Motorola chairman at the time, is credited with introducing *Six Sigma* methodologies for the first time in the early 1980s. This new approach brought more than $16 billion in savings to the company. But it wasn't until 1988 when Motorola earned a National Quality Award that the secrets of how *Six Sigma* methodologies could be applied were publicly announced.

In 1989 Motorola announced its new quality objective: 3.4 defects per million. Measuring quality by something such as 99% acceptable success rate was no longer sufficient, *Six Sigma* had pushed the quality demand far higher, tightening the standard.

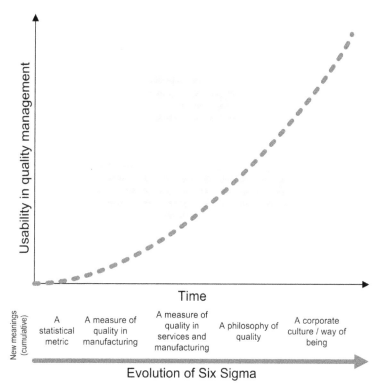

Figure 1.2   The evolution of *Six Sigma*

Soon organisations were claiming that the use of *Six Sigma* was generating savings of the magnitude of:

- more than $12 billion savings over 5 years at General Electric;

- more than $800 million in savings at Honeywell.

According to *iSixSigma Magazine*, during the past 20 years, *Six Sigma* projects saved Fortune 500 companies an estimated $427 billion – the same study found that corporate-wide *Six Sigma* deployments save an average 2 per cent of total revenue per year.[1]

A PHILOSOPHY OF QUALITY AND CORPORATE CULTURE

With such important savings reported by the early adopters of *Six Sigma*, the methodology became more and more sought after by companies in both manufacturing and service industries. Many of these companies have adopted *Six Sigma* principles and concepts as the fundamental philosophy of their corporate cultures.

When *Six Sigma* becomes a philosophy of quality, its meaning is no longer restricted to the simple 3.4 defects per million opportunities metric. The mature *Six Sigma* philosophy aims at implementing organisation-wide empirical, measurement-based strategies for process improvement while embedding itself into the culture of the organisation.

---

1   *iSixSigma Magazine* research – January/February 2007.

SIX SIGMA IN SERVICES

As the methodology was initially developed in manufacturing, there has always been some debate on whether or not *Six Sigma* has applicability in service industries. However, one of the most widely used examples of high sigma capability that is probably even 'seven sigma' compliant is from the service industry: safety of air transportation. The same *Six Sigma* principles that make air travel a high sigma service can be applied to other services within the appropriate cost restraints.

One of the key differences between manufacturing environments and services is that in manufacturing the products are tangible and can be stored and inspected for quality assurance before they reach the client. However, services are delivered in real time and can not be stored or inspected before they reach the client.

Therefore, it becomes imperative that the process by which the service is delivered is designed and tested before it is rolled out to internal or external customers. Service processes must be made robust and foolproof. *Six Sigma* methodologies and a process-focused approach to service design are perfect tools for achieving this goal.

The role of the individual involved in delivering the service is often much more critical to the success or failure of the outcome than in manufacturing environments which, especially in automated factories, usually depends more on machines than on human interaction. Any process whose output is largely dependent on human performance is a process that runs a high risk of having a significant variance, which means that it's hard to control and predict. The human element cannot be eliminated from most service delivery processes, but these processes can be engineered in such a way as to maximise performance. Some common ways to do this in service environments include:

- automating as much of the process as possible – using automated workflows, validation procedures and other service automation solutions. A process that is backed up by technology can also support the individuals involved to perform better and ultimately deliver an outstanding service;

- eliminating inefficient, non value-adding steps in a process – opportunities for defects are directly proportional to the number of steps in the process;

- eliminating bottlenecks within the process;

- using well-defined procedures and processes and training the staff who perform these activities to a very competent level;

- facilitating a good flow of information between all parties involved in the process (clients, stakeholders, employees, and so on);

- standardising the process so that the same way of delivering service is achieved in different locations by different teams.

These are just a few of the general principles that are typically applied in service process improvement projects. *Six Sigma* helps to pinpoint exactly what needs to be done for the process to improve, without wasting resources, whilst at the same time offering an empirical, quantitative view of the performance of the process and highlighting improvement opportunities.

SIX SIGMA IN HR TRANSFORMATION

The chief aim of this book is to explain some of the basic concepts of *Six Sigma* and to show how *Six Sigma* tools and methodologies can be used to manage the practical challenges of improving HR operations, to meet customer expectations at a lower cost and with greater efficiency.

To help illustrate some of the key messages in this book there are examples drawn from Orion Partners' work using *Six Sigma* tools that have been pulled together into a single case study – U Corporation – showing how the tools and methods presented in each section can be used in practice. Although this is a fictional organisation the issues and data used have been derived from Orion Partners' work with international organisations over the last 7 years, and have drawn extensively on the experience of our team of black-belts in using *Six Sigma* to drive HR transformation.

Below is an overview of U Corporation and the scope of the *Six Sigma* project used as a case study:

Case Study – Part I
Background Information

U Corporation engages in the exploration, production, transportation and sale of crude oil and natural gas as well as other petrochemicals. The company operates 250 drilling sites and 3 refineries in Europe, the Americas and the Middle East.

In December 2007 the total number of employees was 75,600 located in 5 countries.

20 months ago, the company created an HR Shared Services Centre (HRSSC) in London as a part of its business transformation process.

Serving over 85 per cent of the total full time workforce, or over 64,000 employees, the centre processes over 9,000 HR queries per month (>108,000 per year).

Being an industrial services company, most of its employees don't have either the skills necessary to access the online self-service or available workstations from which they can access self-service channels. Therefore the most widely used contact channel of the HRSSC is the phone (see Figure 1.3).

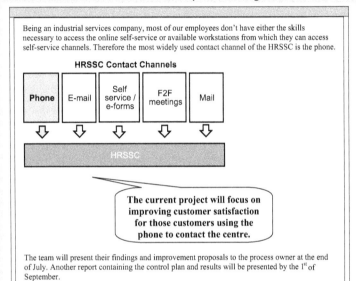

Being an industrial services company, most of our employees don't have either the skills necessary to access the online self-service or available workstations from which they can access self-service channels. Therefore the most widely used contact channel of the HRSSC is the phone.

HRSSC Contact Channels

| Phone | E-mail | Self service / e-forms | F2F meetings | Mail |

HRSSC

The current project will focus on improving customer satisfaction for those customers using the phone to contact the centre.

The team will present their findings and improvement proposals to the process owner at the end of July. Another report containing the control plan and results will be presented by the 1st of September.

Process importance

The high level "Query Management Process" of the HRSSC is of vital importance to our HR function and the organisation as a whole, as it manages and resolves most of the employee and line manager queries (>80%) for all HR areas such as:

- recruitment administration;
- pay and benefits administration;
- pensions administration;
- payroll administration;
- absence and leavers administration;
- employee data management;
- learning and development administration;
- fleet administration.

Figure 1.3   HRSSC contact channels

(2) *Six Sigma* Teams, Projects and Techniques

'The ability to learn faster than your competitors may be the only sustainable competitive advantage.'

Arie De Geus, Royal Dutch/Shell

The *Six Sigma* philosophy borrows part of its terminology from martial arts, offering awards in levels of accomplishment with titles such as masters, champions and black belts, green belts and yellow belts. These titles are deliberately chosen to suggest the many similarities that *Six Sigma* and martial arts have, namely:

- one of the main aims of both *Six Sigma* and martial arts is improvement (self-improvement or the improvement of one's organisation, products, and so on);

- in both, personal and organisational discipline is of the highest importance;

- both require the acquisition and deployment of substantial knowledge and expertise.

The *Six Sigma* teams are usually formed within the organisation and are composed of members from different functional backgrounds and levels of experience. The common aim of team members is to improve the quality of the products or services that their organisation offers. To enhance facilitation and positive team dynamics, the structure of *Six Sigma* teams is designed to include mentors, coaches, process experts and facilitators, as well as subject matter experts with particular deep technical or functional skills (for example, reward or compensation and benefits experts).

Most *Six Sigma* projects are led by *master black belts*. These are highly qualified *Six Sigma* experts in charge of the strategic coordination of projects within the organisation. They also act as mentors to black and green belts and are qualified to teach others the methodologies and tools of *Six Sigma*.

The next level of the *Six Sigma* hierarchy are the *black belts*, also experts in the tools and methodologies used, the black belts act as team leaders and are responsible for the implementation of process improvement projects within the organisation. They work full time on these projects and act as mentors themselves to the green belts, and also as facilitators for the team as a whole. Experience of applying *Six Sigma* over more than 20 years indicates that a single black belt alone can bring an estimated $1 million per year in savings to an organisation, if they are given sufficient responsibility and authority to act.

The *green* and *yellow belts* are employees who have basic skills and knowledge of *Six Sigma* tools and work on or lead process improvement projects but on a part-time basis, while still maintaining their usual day job. However, even if their *Six Sigma* knowledge is limited to the basics they are usually experts in their field of work. Their deep process and technical knowledge is pivotal to the success of the *Six Sigma* programme.

In some organisations, there are also subject matter experts similar to green belts, called *yellow belts*, who have knowledge of *Six Sigma* methods and work on projects but can not lead them. Often, yellow belts as experts in their own fields identify potential improvement opportunities that are then escalated by green and black belts to become *Six Sigma* projects.

In an HR function it is helpful to have a number of yellow or green belts trained who work in your transactional and process teams. A black belt would be most helpful in a project lead role, bringing their specialist skills to projects being run in the HR function and those run by HR, e.g. organisational changes.

SIX SIGMA PROJECTS AND ACTIVITIES

Six Sigma teams often play the role of internal consultants within an organisation. Common activities include workshops, interviews, focus groups, team meetings, and more individual tasks such as data gathering, processing of statistical data, computing indicators and mapping and understanding trends and the root cause of errors and process failures. One of the requirements for success in *Six Sigma* projects is a team leader who ensures that individual analysis is shared and understood across the team.

SIX SIGMA TOOLS AND TECHNIQUES

Being in essence an approach based on wide involvement, *Six Sigma* uses a variety of tools and techniques borrowed from areas such as business consultancy, statistics and even marketing, to collect, analyse and use information to design and implement process improvements.

The best known element of *Six Sigma* is its focus on empirical methods based on statistics and quantitative data. For these, a wide range of statistical tools are used such as distributions, descriptive statistics or more advanced ones such as various methods for analysing fluctuations or uncertainty within a process.

However, process improvement projects are complex and cannot be limited simply to the quantitative dimension, so *Six Sigma* also uses qualitative tools to capture data and insights which are not numerically based.

In Table 2.1 we can see a few of the tools generally used in *Six Sigma* projects, categorised by type and the stages where they are best applied.

Using *Six Sigma* tools, in particular in HR Transformation, provides a means of structuring and managing your project so that it runs smoothly. Most importantly, it creates a project approach which is specifically designed to ensure excellence in future service delivery. The stages described above (DMAIC) will be discussed in more detail in the next chapter.

Table 2.1 Summary of the tools commonly used in *Six Sigma* projects

Type of tool/technique			Example deliverables	6σ Stage*	Example tools
Data collection	**Quantitative**		Quantitative data Number of defects	D, M, C	Surveys Automated data collection tools Check sheets (e.g. defect check sheets) Group voting
	Qualitative		Customer opinions (qualitative)	D	Focus groups Interviews Workshops
Data analysis	**Quantitative**	**Graphical**	Distribution charts Patterns/trends identified	A,C	Control charts Run charts Capability analysis Pareto charts Scatter plots Box plots
		Numerical (statistics)	Statistical indicators	A	ANOVA Capability indices Sigma level
	Qualitative		Well organized qualitative information Clarity	D,A	7M tools (affinity diagrams, interrelationship diagrams, etc.)
Creativity/Idea generation			New ideas Solutions to problems	D, M, A, I	Brain storming Nominal group technique THE (Technology/ Human/Environment) Six Thinking Hats
Knowledge discovery			Causes of problems	A	Ishikawa tool 5 Whys
Formalising/ Communication			Clear communications Plans	D,M,C	Project charter Process documentation Operational definitions Gantt charts Flow charts SIPOC Dashboards
Simulation/Testing			Quantitative data on potential system/ process behaviour	I	Monte Carlo simulations Pilot tests
Change management			Change management plans/roadmaps Risk assessment Internal communications	I,C	Force field analysis SSC (Stop, Start, Continue)

*   Stage refers to some of the stages where the respective types of tools are used most often. The stages are: D = Define, M = Measure, A = Analyse, I = Improve, C = Control.

③ *Six Sigma* Methodologies

> 'In world-class organisations, working to improve quality is not an extracurricular activity. It is a minimum requirement.'
>
> Chang, Labovitz, and Rosansky, authors, *Making Quality Work: A Leadership Guide for the Results-Driven Manager*

Six Sigma methodologies are data driven problem-solving processes that aim at reducing defects or errors. At the highest level the *Six Sigma* approach is organised into five consecutive stages, each having specific goals, tasks and deliverables. These are summarised as DMAIC, which stands for:

- define;

- measure;

- analyse;

- improve;

- control.

In some projects the final two stages will differ and instead of 'improve' and 'control' the phases are 'design' and 'verify'. (DMADV).

Figure 3.1 shows the two main (DMAIC and DMADV) approaches to *Six Sigma* improvements.

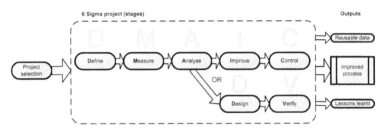

Figure 3.1   Stages of a *Six Sigma* project

The DMAIC methodology is a key approach to process improvement, however, it is not suitable for every project. Usually we can apply a DMAIC approach in cases where the process improvement project meets the following criteria:

1. It is complex and the causes of the problem are not completely known e.g. high payroll error rates where multiple systems are used to generate payroll data.

2. There is judged to be enough room for improvement to make the project worthwhile investing time and effort e.g. reducing recruitment time to hire.

3. There is no obvious or predetermined solution available – if you already know how to solve the problem then just do it. However, sometimes the obvious solution is merely a quick-fix that masks the true underlying problem e.g. low customer satisfaction scores relating to the HR Shared Service Centre.

DMADV, as the second is used less often and is relevant when there is a requirement to design new processes. This may be when a new operation, such as a centralised HR Shared Service Centre or a new e-recruitment approach is being implemented, or when the original processes are so badly fragmented that a complete new design is needed.

Sometimes a project starts out with a DMAIC approach but it then becomes obvious that a complete redesign of the process is required. Thus it is possible for projects to switch from DMAIC to DMADV especially during the analysis phase.In the remainder of this book we focus on the tools and techniques used in each stage of DMAIC. The Design and Verify stages apply much more to situations where a technical process is going to be re-tooled (remembering that *Six Sigma* emerged from manufacturing). When we apply *Six Sigma* to a transformation process, we are looking to generate improvement in a service which we can then control, so we will focus in this book on these stages of the *Six Sigma* methodology.

Frequently HR Transformation projects miss certain key steps which could make the project ultimately more effective because the approach taken has insufficient structure. For example, deciding the solution to recruitment cycle time issues is improved technology before properly analysing the problem (missing the 'analyse' phase) can result in a high technology spend when the real issue was lack of training in the recruitment process.

DEFINE

As the initial phase, the Define stage is when the team is formed and the project's scope and goals are defined and incorporated in a project charter.

Forming the *Six Sigma* team is usually the responsibility of the black or green belt that initiated and leads the project. During this stage, the project leader will assess the needs of the project in order to identify what it demands in terms of skills and specific experience and then to source the best possible team members. The assessment should ensure that the members are chosen such that all the skills needed to successfully complete the project are covered. For example in an HR environment, a process improvement project would work best if the team had the proper set of skills/competencies, including:

- subject matter expertise in the various HR activities;

- knowledge of business policies and procedures;

- previous experience with *Six Sigma* projects;

- a willingness to take part in improvement projects;

- leadership skills;

- communication/presentation/facilitation skills.

Figure 3.2 gives a summary of the key steps in the define phase.

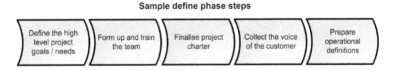

Figure 3.2   Sample Define Phase Steps

To help define the overall project goals the following questions are asked:

- who are the customers/stakeholders? What are their needs/ expectations?

- what is the exact scope of the project?

- what deliverables will be produced by the end of the project?

- what are the processes to be improved?

- what are the known defects or error rates?

This helps bring clarity and enhances communication both inside the team and with other stakeholders.

The deliverables of the define phase usually include:

- a Project Charter summarising the scope and key milestones, risks and deliverables;

- a fully formed and trained team ready to work on the project;

- a high-level process map (SIPOC (Suppliers – Inputs – Process – Outputs – Customers) summary – see p. 30 or flowchart);

- clear definitions of defects, critical characteristics;

- project management documentation (Gantt chart, actions list, roles, and so on).

In many transformation projects, this is also the stage at which a business case will be produced. This is not a prime feature of the *Six Sigma* methodology however, as traditional *Six Sigma* projects have been about process improvement in factory environments where investment has not always been needed to make the change. However completing the deliverables noted above will provide much of the information you would require in a business case, with the addition of the financial measures attached to them.

PROJECT CHARTER

The Project Charter is an essential communication tool for any *Six Sigma* project.

The Project Charter should include information such as:

- project title;

- the goals of the project;

- a description of the problem that the project will solve and how this problem currently affects the organisation;

- a summary of the scope of the project and a brief overview of the deliverables that will be produced;

- a list of team members (sponsor, leaders, experts);

- a summary of the key stakeholders who need to be influenced and informed;

- a summary of the resources needed to undertake the project;

- an estimate of the duration of the project;

- a summary of the business case for undertaking the project;

- a brief risks and mitigations analysis.

This is not an exhaustive list and each organisation will usually use its own project charter template. The important thing is that it should contain all the necessary information to ensure that it is a useful communication tool to align and organise the project team and wider stakeholders.

During the initial stages of the project, the project charter may undergo reviews and revisions. A typical evolution of the document may include:

1. Black belt drafts the charter together with the yellow belt who proposed the new improvement project as subject matter expert (in HR the yellow belt could be a highly skilled HR employee such as an HR Business Partner or HR functional specialist).

2. Master black belt reviews the charter and makes any necessary amendments or suggestions.

3. The black belt finishes the first draft of the charter and builds the business case for the project – usually together with other project proposals.

4. Potential improvement projects are presented to the stakeholders (sponsors) and projects are selected.

5. HR executive-level sponsors review/agree with the initial version of the charter.

6. The charter is again reviewed and a final version is produced together with the project management documentation. Also, as the team is formed, its final structure is added to the charter during the define phase.

An example project charter for our main case study on HRSSC service delivery can be found in Appendix 1.

COLLECTING THE VOICE OF THE CUSTOMER (VOC)

An important element of the Define phase is to gather information from and about the customers of the service HR is looking to improve. Customer focus is at the core of any quality management initiative. Knowing who our customers are and their needs and expectations is an obvious condition of business success and an ultimate goal of any *Six Sigma* project.

Within the HR function determining customer needs is just as important as in any other commercial activity. Customer satisfaction surveys, interviews and focus groups are just a few techniques that HR can use to get better information on the voice of customers. The results of such endeavours will help *Six Sigma* teams to better shape the concept of quality that they must define in their project.

Many organisations already collect information on employee satisfaction with HR through yearly surveys or focus groups, or sometimes they hire external consultants to assess how HR is seen through the organisation. However, often this data is high level and does not dive deeply enough into the differing performance of services within the HR function.

Since *Six Sigma* is a process improvement philosophy, it requires more detailed process-specific data regarding the voice and needs of HR customers than is usually provided by standard customer surveys. The project team will define the questions which need to be answered and decide on the appropriate tool to use. For example, if we are planning to improve the recruitment process of a company in the construction sector, we would be interested in data such as:

- what are the main issues in recruitment within the industry?

- what levels of satisfaction do line mangers have with the recruitment services provided by HR?

- how would line managers see a better recruitment service?

- what are the critical quality factors for line managers when recruiting people through HR in this particular case? Is it cost, the ability to fill positions quickly or the quality of the new employees? Or a combination of all three?

The four most widely used methods for collecting the voice of customer are interviews, focus-groups, workshops and surveys.

The first three methods are most useful when dealing with a small number of people, with a need to collect qualitative data. Surveys are most efficient when you need to collect more quantitative data from a large number of people.

The following part of the case study shows briefly how the voice of the customer was collected and stakeholder needs assessed in an HR Shared Services Centre (HRSSC).

Case Study – Part II (Define)

D.1   Collecting VOC

The 'voice of the customer' (VOC) was collected in order to find information on four key elements:

1.   Percentage of employees who used the services of the HRSSC.

2.   The overall level of satisfaction that the customers currently have with the service.

3.   Most important customer requirements.

4.   Possible improvements (customer suggestions).

The team chose to use questionnaires and interviews to collate this data.

D.1.1   Questionnaires

A single page questionnaire was distributed to a representative number of employees that had been using the services of the HRSSC.

The questionnaires were targeted to those customers using the services of the centre for employee services.

D.1.2   VOC Conclusions

After analysing the data collated, the team arrived at the following conclusions:

1.   32 per cent of the employees had used the services of the HRSSC in the past 3 months. This figure was significantly higher than the industry average.

2.   67 per cent of the employees had accessed the HRSSC services using the telephone. This confirmed that, since the company's activities were mainly industrial, most employees didn't have either the necessary skills to access web or intranet self-services, or access to a computer and Internet while at work.

3.   As seen in Figure 3.3 most calls made to the HRSSC during the past 3 months were payroll and benefits queries.

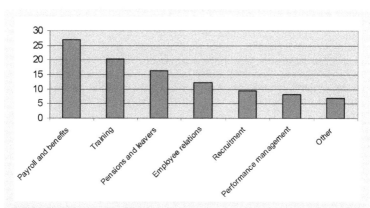

**Figure 3.3   Services used by customers in the past
3 months**

Such a high demand for these services was not a normal occurrence and
this prompted the team to examine the root causes.

The customer satisfaction rating, which was the most important overall
result of the survey, showed a clear bias towards low ratings, and proved
that the customer satisfaction for this particular HRSSC was much lower
than the industry average, see Figure 3.4.

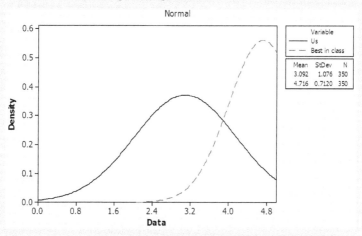

Figure 3.4   Our customer satisfaction vs. best in class

D.2   Main stakeholders' needs

The team also defined the needs of all three major groups of stakeholders, in order to make sure later in the analysis and improvement phases that the improvements implemented to raise customer satisfaction (the scope of the project), would not interfere negatively with the needs of other groups of stakeholders.

Table 3.1   Needs of different stakeholders

Customers	Shareholders	HRSSC employees
• fast and easy access;	• low cost per call;	• user-friendly HRMS interface;
• professional service;	• low rate of returned calls;	• good communications and cooperation with other teams and managers.
• first call clearance;	• efficiency;	
• human interaction – minimise automated answers.	• high customer satisfaction levels.	

MAPPING THE PROCESS

Along with understanding the customer and their needs in the process, the Define phase also looks to map the existing process. This can help HR functions to really get to the root of what the problem might be, before looking at solutions.

Process maps drawn up based on all the steps required to transform a set of inputs into the outputs of the process. High level process maps give an overview of all the key steps that are required to create the outputs but without all the detailed activities. In *Six Sigma* projects these are usually used to define the scope of the project. See table opposite.

Suppliers	Inputs	Process	Outputs	Customers
All suppliers relevant to the process	Inputs needed for the process to be performed	A high-level map of the process	The outputs that the process generates	Customers of the process

Low-level process maps are more detailed and show as many actions as possible, frequently down to desktop activity level. At this level of detail processes are usually mapped as flowcharts that are used in the later stages of the *Six Sigma* project to determine the causes of defects and make any improvements necessary to the process.

SIPOC

A good approach to high-level process mapping in *Six Sigma* is to develop a SIPOC diagram (SIPOC stands for Suppliers – Inputs – Process – Outputs – Customers). This diagram is useful during the define phase as it helps clarify the five essential elements of the process.

As the SIPOC diagram contains a high-level process map, this will represent just the main components, usually linearly, avoiding iterations or conditions. See Table 3.2.

The SIPOC tool helps HR functions clarify all the parties and processes involved in the area they want to transform. This ensures that, in planning the changes to be made, all affected areas can be taken into account.

Table 3.2   Using the SIPOC tool

High-level query management				
Suppliers	**Inputs**	**Process**	**Outputs**	**Customers**
HRMS supplier Consultants CoEs	Customer ID information Customer queries (information)	Answer call Gather caller info Validate caller info Transfer call Search advice info on Knowledge Base Deliver advice Log query details	Solutions Advice Updates to HRMS	Employees Line managers Middle/ senior managers

FLOW CHARTING

Another process mapping tool, used for lower-level mapping, is flow charting. This is one of the most important tools as it helps standardise processes, communicate, spot bottlenecks and improve the process. Today it is very common for most medium to large organisations to have detailed process maps represented as flowcharts in their process documentation.

A flow chart is actually just a simple map of the process where each task, decision or sub-process is represented using standardised shapes that are then connected in chronological order. When building a flow chart it is good practice to differentiate the tasks that are assigned to different departments or employees by using swim lanes as seen in the example on page 37.

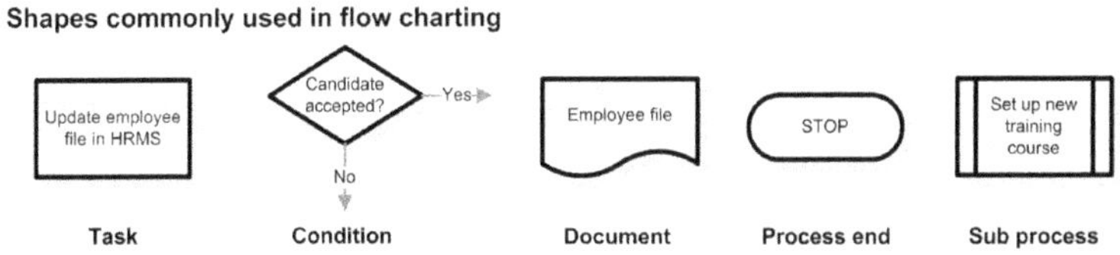

Shapes commonly used in flow charting

| Task | Condition | Document | Process end | Sub process |

Figure 3.5 **Shapes commonly used in flow charting**

In the *Six Sigma* DMAIC methodology, flow charts are used mainly in the Define and Analyse phases for the following purposes:

● to standardise the process;

● to enhance clear communication of the process map;

● to help the team improve the process by studying the workflow;

● process reengineering;

● determining the location of potential defects within the workflow.

An example of how a flowchart can be used to highlight defects and map the process in an HRSSC query management process can be seen in the second part of the main case study later in this chapter.

Whilst it is important to understand current processes, in our experience, current process mapping can be a rabbit hole down which many HR Transformation projects can lose substantial time and resources. Make sure that you spend only a minimum amount of effort on this step, using it to be certain of where the areas for improvement are, rather than to create detailed, end to end current process maps.

CRITICAL CHARACTERISTICS OF PRODUCTS OR SERVICES

Before commencing activity that may change a process, it is necessary to establish what must stay the same, where the biggest change impact will be and what aspects of the process are critical for your business. The critical characteristics of products or services can be divided into 3 categories:

- critical to customer/stakeholder;

- critical to cost;

- critical to schedule.

In an ideal world products and services would perform at six or higher sigma levels for all these categories. However, in the real world the cost of achieving this would be prohibitive in terms of resources, time and investment and so a trade-off that is consistent with the overall HR strategy must be established.

The measurable characteristics of a product or service that are key to satisfying the needs of customers and stakeholders are called 'critical to quality' or CTQs (see Figure 3.6). For the *Six Sigma* team, it is important to identify what these characteristics are as early as possible during the define phase, as knowing what our CTQs are will help us in planning the measurement phase.

The other two main categories of critical factors are CTC and CTS. CTC stands for 'critical to cost', and includes those measurable characteristics that would have a strong impact on reducing the costs, while CTS includes those 'critical-to-schedule' ones that have a great impact on the time it takes to deliver a product or service.

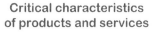

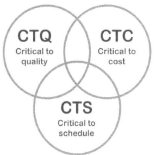

**Figure 3.6   Critical   characteristics   of   products   and
services**

These three categories are not rigid, and elements can be
included in two or even all three at the same time. The
example in our main case study (time to solve queries) is a
characteristic critical to all three – quality, cost and schedule.
Thus the time to solve (or resolve) queries is often a key
performance indicator (KPI) in HR Shared Services.

It is useful to differentiate when a category is critical on two or
more dimensions as this stresses the importance of focusing
on this variable as a key to overall service improvement.
Mapping the different elements and variables on a Venn
diagram similar to the one in Figure 3.6 is helpful when trying
to communicate critical characteristics. It helps the team to
really concentrate on issues that will make a difference.

Sometimes the variables or KPIs that measure these characteristics
are obvious. For example we know that customers expect
their queries to be dealt with quickly as a CTQ for the query
management process, so it is vital to measure the current 'time
to solve query' activities. Often though, the characteristics that
the customers demand are of a more qualitative nature, such as

'I want the answers to my queries to be rigorous and professional yet also easy to understand'. In such cases the *Six Sigma* team must find metrics through which they can transform this qualitative requirement into a quantitative, measurable variable. In this particular case, surveys using Likert scales (that is, Strongly Agree to Strongly Disagree ratings) to assess the perceived professionalism and clarity of answers by customers can be useful.

Later, in the Measure phase, we will see how critical factors can be linked to metrics and help us develop our measurement plan.

DEFINING THE DEFECTS

Defects are undesired results in the performance of a product or service that fail to meet customer or stakeholder requirements.

The quest of the *Six Sigma* team is to minimise defects by finding the root causes and eliminating them. But, in order to minimise them, we must first define the defects and be clear what we are working on. Some examples of defects in the HR function that could be minimised through *Six Sigma* projects would include:

- shared services queries not answered within agreed service levels;

- wrong payslips sent out to employees;

- fulfilment of vacancies taking longer than specified;

- performance appraisals being completed long after the target date;

- errors in personal data held on the HR system undermining reporting;

- joining instructions for training courses not being sent out on time;

- additional monthly pay elements being missed before the payroll cut-off date each month.

Defects must be defined against how they relate to the critical characteristics to gain a better perspective on the impact they have. Knowing the importance of the types of possible defects can help prioritise them and optimise the use of resources invested in improving the process.

For each type of defect the *Six Sigma* team will develop clear, measurable definitions to make sure that all parties engaged in the process have the same understanding of what the defects are. Lack of clarity in this area can lead to errors in measurement that cascade down through the whole project.

In defining the defects, additional tools such as process mapping can be used to get an in-depth understanding of where defects may occur within the process. Such an approach can be seen in the next part of the case study.

Case Study – Part III (Define)

D.3. Defining the Defects

The scope of this project was to improve the HR Shared Services Centre (HRSSC) customer satisfaction mainly by reducing the time needed to solve phone queries, in particular by reducing the number of hand offs. The process for handling queries can be seen in Figure 3.7. We can identify three possible main defect types that fall within this scope:

- call duration >6 minutes – any call with a duration (excluding queue waiting time) that exceeded 6 minutes;

- not a first call clearance or hand off – any call for which the query was not resolved at the time of call (either the operator or customer has to call back at a later time) or is handed off to another operator;

- queue waiting time >30 seconds.

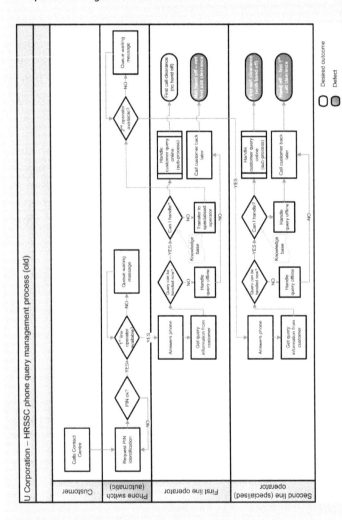

Figure 3.7   Query management process map (old)

DEFINING OPPORTUNITIES

As well as understanding what the defects are, an assessment needs to be made showing where in the process the opportunities for defects to occur are. This enables the HR transformation to focus on the areas of most impact when improving the process.

In *Six Sigma* opportunities are formally classified as the number of chances that a defect will occur per unit. In manufacturing environments, units are the products produced while in services it is the 'service' produced at the end of a process.

For example, in our case study the full process of query management, from the time the customer initiated the call to the time when the query is closed, is considered a unit of service in the HRSSC. One unit of service can have one or more defects at the same time. In a worst case scenario, there may be the maximum number of defects possible in just one query: the query's duration exceeds 6 minutes, it is handed off and the customer had to wait more than 30 seconds in the queue. So here, one unit, the query, has three opportunities for defects.

DPMO stands for defects per million opportunities observed.

$$\frac{\text{Defects per unit}}{\text{Opportunities / unit}} \times 1\ 000\ 000 = \text{DPMO}$$

Sometimes people get confused and consider a product or unit of service to be the same as an opportunity – this leads to statements such as '*Six Sigma* level means having a maximum 3.4 broken products in 1 million produced' – when actually one product unit produced can have 100 opportunities for defects to occur. This is why units produced and opportunities are two entirely different concepts. The same is valid for services. There may be 10,000 HR queries per month at U Corporation, but the opportunities for defects are multiple for each query, leading to a much higher total number of opportunities.

For HR Transformation, defining the opportunities means gaining a full understanding of the weak points in your HR process. For instance, the fact that in a recruitment process the cycle time can be long, but is lengthened by a combination of both the HR side of the process and the line manager inputs to the process, both of which must be addressed if significant improvement is to be achieved. At the end of the Define phase the team will have a deep understanding of all the possible causes of the problem they are trying to solve, and can move on to understanding the scale of the different elements of the problem.

MEASURE

The measurement phase is a natural continuation of the Define phase. We continue with data collection but now the data we need is usually more quantitative in nature. During this phase we seek to collect the quantitative information regarding the inner workings of the process or processes that we're trying to improve (see Figure 3.8).

Sample measurement phase steps

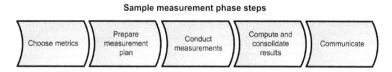

Figure 3.8   Sample measurement phase steps

Measurement should aim to gather enough information needed to paint the full picture of the current situation. *Six Sigma* teams are also well advised to recall the statement by Albert Einstein that 'not everything that counts can be counted; not everything that can be counted counts'. Project teams need to agree and differentiate what really counts from what is just measurable.

The deliverables of this phase include:

- the list of measures (identified and defined);

- measurement (data collection) plan;

- results of the measurement process:

  - process variation,

  - Xs and Ys (input/output variables),

  - sigma level calculated.

SELECTING THE METRICS

Selecting the appropriate metrics can have a decisive effect on the outcome of any *Six Sigma* project. The metrics can be either relevant and offer a valuable view of the performance or, conversely, poorly chosen and complicate the problem further, causing a waste of time and resources.

Two major pitfalls have been known to lure *Six Sigma* teams into the dark side of process measurements, these are:

- over-engineering measurement or, collecting too much irrelevant information. The efficacy of a corporate dashboard or *Six Sigma* measurement plan is not measured by the number of metrics it contains, but by the quality of insight that those metrics offer;

- using data just because it exists. The fact that some data already exists does not mean that it is necessarily the most valid and useful data. In many cases pre-existing data that is limited or of dubious accuracy may merely serve to limit the search of root causes and lead to too narrow a range of options thereby making the project self-defeating.

The trick to avoiding such pitfalls is to select the metrics based on the original project objectives. It is also useful to compare how other organisations measure similar processes/service activities as part of a benchmarking exercise.

METRICS SELECTION MATRIX

Once the potential metrics and critical to quality factors are known, a matrix can be built to explore which of the metrics have the greatest impact on quality. In the case study, the *Six Sigma* team used this tool to find the relative importance of proposed metrics with the results as shown in Figure 3.9.

To create a metrics selection matrix follow the steps below:

- list the proposed input variables (X's) on the columns of the matrix;

- list the customer requirements or output variables (Y's) on the rows;

- add a weight to each output variable according to how important it is for the customer;

Case Study – Part IV (Measure)

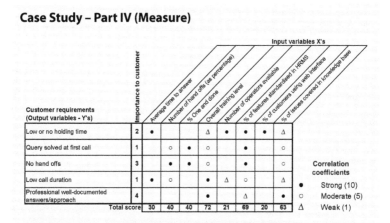

The matrix contains:

Customer requirements (Output variables - Y's)	Importance to customer	Average time to answer	Number of hand offs (as percentage)	% One and done	Overall training level	Number of operators available	% of features standardised in HRMS	% of customers using web interface	% of issues covered in knowledge base	
Low or no holding time	2	●		Δ	●	●	●	Δ		
Query solved at first call	1		○	●	○		●		○	
No hand offs	3		●	●	○		●		○	
Low call duration	1	●	○		●	Δ	○		Δ	
Professional well-documented answers/approach	4				●		Δ		●	
Total score		30	40	40	72	21	69	20	63	

Input variables X's

Correlation coefficients
- ● Strong (10)
- ○ Moderate (5)
- Δ Weak (1)

Figure 3.9   A matrix for assessing the impact of a range of customer variables

After collecting the critical to quality factors, the team created the above metrics selection matrix that was used in order to develop the data collection plan and help focus on the most important variables.

- work through the matrix and add ratings representing how strong the correlation between the respective input and output variables is;

- compute the total score for each input variable using a weighted sum.

The higher the total score of an input variable, the higher its impact on the customer satisfaction. After the total scores have been computed they can be presented as a Pareto chart to highlight the relative importance of each of the variables. Refer to Figure 3.30 for further details regarding Pareto charts. This process allows the team to quickly assess the areas which will have the greatest impact on process improvement.

The metrics selection process used in the following section of the case study, together with its outputs, shows how process-specific metrics can be chosen and collected in *Six Sigma* projects.

Case Study – Part V (Measure)

M.1   Selecting HRSSC Metrics

In Figure 3.10 we can see the relative impact that each of the purpose metrics had on customer satisfaction.

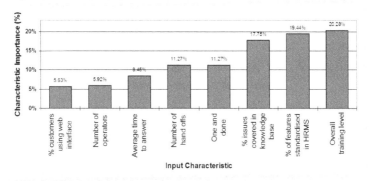

Figure 3.10   Metrics selection matrix results

In most service delivery organisations, the overall competence of the team was the most important input variable.

The number of customers using the web interface (self-service) was not as important at this point since the scope of the project was limited to improving the process just for phone queries. However, it did affect the overall work loading level of the contact centre as calls were more costly to handle than work completed mainly over 'self-service' technologies.

The following variables were selected to be used in the project:

	Variable name	Description	Collection method
1	Average time to answer (Queue time)	Holding time until first available operator can answer	Automatic – using data from switch

	Variable name	Description	Collection method
2	% hand offs	% of queries that needed to be handed off to other operators or support teams *(target: <20%)*	Manual – collected by green belts (using data collection, DC, tool)
3	% One and done	% of queries resolved at first call	Manual – collected by green belts (DC, tool)
4	Call duration	Average duration of calls (time between operator answer and call termination)	Manual – collected by green belts (DC, tool)
5	Query complexity	1–5 rating of query complexity	Manual – collected by green belts (DC, tool)
6	Overall training level	The overall training level is measured through a series of assessments made by the employees themselves and their managers, on different skills related to their job	Through online assessment tools
7	Number of operators	Total number of operators in the HRSSC	Information available
8	% features standardised in the HRMS	% of the processes used that are standardised and can be dealt with directly by the HRSSC operators	Black belt and green belt will calculate this figure
9	% customers using web interface	% of employees who use the web interface or intranet self-services	Web statistics on online account utilisation & phone pin stats
10	% issues covered in the knowledge base	% of the issues for which information was readily available in the internal knowledge base or HRMS	Black belt & green belt will calculate this figure
11	Outbound call category	Category of outbound call (supplier call, internal, technical support, and so on)	Manual – collected by green belts (DC Tool)

At this point we identified that the data needed for our analysis fell into 3 main categories:

1. Data already available.

2. Data that could be computed from available data.

3. Data that needed to be collected.

STATISTICAL CONCEPTS IN SIX SIGMA

'Statistical thinking will one day be as necessary for efficient citizenship as the ability to read and write.'

H. G. Wells

Much of the *Six Sigma* philosophy is based on empirical facts and analyses generated by the application of a whole range of statistical tools and techniques. However, *Six Sigma* is not simply an empirical, scientific approach. Many softer skills are also used to enhance creativity, collect data and help generate the best possible solutions. The following section focuses on the statistical concepts, creative analysis tools can be found from page 77 onwards.

A *Six Sigma* team should possess both the statistical and the softer skills needed to successfully conduct their process improvement or design projects. Having this mix of skills in an HR Transformation project is vital. This will make sure your project team can analyse the problem and design solutions based on both quantitative and qualitative measures, and create detailed analysis at the same time as really being able to engage with the organisation on the change.

The rest of this section outlines some of the key statistical concepts used in *Six Sigma*, from the most basic ones like variables or ranges through to full blown statistical control analyses. To illustrate the main points we will use the query management process in the HRSSC in U Corporation together with a number of other examples.

Input and output variables

From a quantitative standpoint, *Six Sigma* treats processes as mathematical functions that have input and output variables.

The input variables are called Xs while output variables Ys. The origin of this terminology is the mathematical expression of a function such as:

$$Y_1 = f_{(x_1, x_2, \ldots, x_n)}$$

To illustrate this, we can consider for example a recruitment process, illustrated in Figure 3.11:

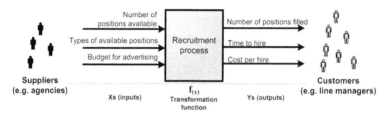

Figure 3.11   The recruitment process

The process can be viewed as a transformation function that turns the inputs into outputs. The performance of the process will always be quantified by its outputs or Ys. In the above example we could determine whether the respective recruitment process met customer requirements (or not) by analysing its outputs against the SLAs (or the defined list of defects that we've built by studying the needs of our customers). It is helpful to identify enough outputs (Ys) so that we can measure the impact of our processes in terms of both customers and other stakeholders.

In this example, the line managers are the customers who need vacancies to be filled. The line managers are mainly interested in the time it takes HR to find appropriate candidates and the percentage of vacant positions filled within the agreed target timeframe. Other customers (such as senior management and shareholders) might focus on the relative costs per hire.

One of the main tasks of *Six Sigma* teams is to improve process outcomes and at the same time balance the improvement against the often different needs of both stakeholders and customers so that an appropriate equilibrium is maintained.

The inputs are also important in helping to identify the root causes of any problems in service delivery. Frequently a root cause is due to one or more of the inputs being insufficient to meet customer needs or to guarantee the smooth execution of the process. In the case of the recruitment process, if the budget is not adequate to advertise the roles, then it is likely that insufficient candidates will be generated to fill all vacancies.

Types of data

In defining the input and output variables, it is important to bear in mind the type of data used to measure each variable as this will drive the selection of data collection methods and the choice of analysis tools.

Generally *Six Sigma* project teams work with continuous or discrete data. Continuous data variables are those that can be measured on a continuous scale, meaning that they can, at least in theory, be infinitely divided into smaller parts to achieve any required level of precision. Examples of continuous data:

- time required to solve queries in the HRSSC;

- cost of hire;

- time to develop and deliver L&D training programmes.

Discrete data variables are those variables that cannot be measured on a continuous scale. Examples of discrete variables within the HR function would include:

- binary data (when we have just two choices; yes or no, true or false):

  - Has the query been responded to within the agreed service levels? – Yes or no?

- fixed data that can be counted:

  - the number of salaries paid incorrectly each month (it is unlikely that we will have 32.4 salaries paid wrongly. The answer will be 32 or 33),

  - the number of hand-offs between different teams in the HRSSC,

  - the number of available HR people on any one shift.

- attribute nominal data – where there is a choice from a limited number of attributes, for example:

  - type of query (Payroll, Flex Bens, and so on),

  - method of query (Phone, e-mail, e-forms).

- attribute ordinal – when the attribute can be ranked on a scale:

  - employee satisfaction levels with HR service (Likert scale: 1 – poor, 2 – fair, 3 – average, 4 – good, 5 – excellent).

In practice it is normal to limit the precision when measuring continuous variables, for example, to seconds for time or, at most, to two decimal points for monetary values. Once the variables and data types relevant to the process have been defined, measurement and analysis of that data can be undertaken, which help the HR transformation team to spot trends in the data.

The basics: ranges, distributions and histograms

To make sense of a series of data *Six Sigma* teams will start with basic tools such as the range, distributions and the use of histograms to help spot trends.

One of the most basic characteristics of quantitative data is the range. The range is the difference between the largest and the smallest scores in any data series. If the highest salary in U Corporation is £1 million and the lowest £20,000 then the range is £980,000.

However, the range by itself gives very little information about the data set. Distributions and histograms are amongst the most powerful data analysis methods in statistics and *Six Sigma* projects, and although they are not much more complicated than the range as concepts, they do help reveal a substantial amount more about a set of data.

A distribution shows how frequently a variable takes a value within the range of the data. For instance, in a salary distribution, the graph will show the number of people who hold each salary, so you can easily spot peaks and clusters in the data. Distributions help *Six Sigma* teams calculate how many opportunities lie within the desired performance limits and how many of those opportunities result in something going wrong or defects. At the sixth sigma level, 99.9997 per cent of observations would have values between the set limits. Distributions can also be used to determine whether or not a process is in the statistically acceptable boundaries of control set by the process owners.

The most common graphical display of a distribution is called a histogram. As seen in Figure 3.12, showing a distribution of salaries in an organisation, a histogram is a bar chart that shows how many data points there are in different sub-ranges. Just by a brief scan of the histogram a process owner can observe some important elements about the data, namely whether the dispersion of a data set is normally distributed or skewed to one end of the data range.

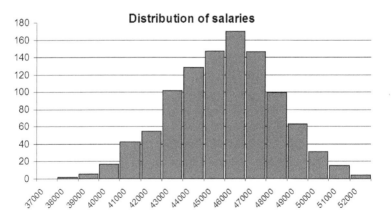

Figure 3.12 A typical histogram

To describe quickly how data is distributed teams may use quantiles. Quantiles are points that divide the range of the data into equal parts. Most people are familiar with the concepts of dividing data into quartiles (four parts) and into deciles (ten parts). Table 3.3 gives some other common quantiles used in *Six Sigma* work.

Table 3.3   Names of different types of quantiles

Number of quantiles	Name
100	Percentiles
20	Vingtiles
12	Duo-deciles
10	Deciles
9	Noniles
5	Quintiles
4	Quartiles

If distributions show how frequently a variable takes a value, cumulative distributions show how much of the data lies below a certain value. By transforming the absolute values to percentages, on the Y axis of a cumulative distribution histogram it is easy to show what percentage of data lies below, or above a given value. In the example shown in Figure 3.13 the cumulative distribution of call durations is shown. This quickly shows that with a target of 50 per cent of calls to have been successfully ended (closed) within 3 minutes then currently more than 50 per cent of the calls are taking over 6 minutes to close.

Using distribution and cumulative distribution charts in the early stages of an HR Transformation project can be particularly useful. By looking at your data in this way you can tell the story about why change needs to happen, for instance, '90 per cent of our training budgets are spent on just 15 per cent of our workforce, leaving us without the investment in talent we need to ensure future growth', these statements come from an analysis of data on distribution charts.

Case study – Part VI (Measure)

M.2   Measure

To take a first glimpse at how the call duration results look we have plotted a cumulative distribution chart (cumulative percentage vs. minutes to close).

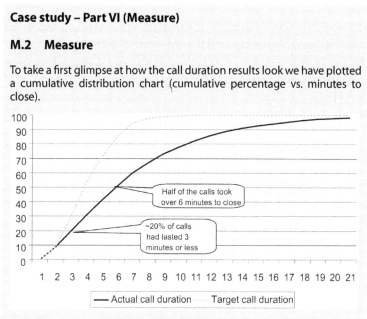

Figure 3.13   Cumulative distribution of call duration

Descriptive statistics   In addition to charts which are useful in data analysis and in producing a visual summary with reports and presentations, there are also numerical indicators that offer information about the data that is being analysed. In the following section, some of these numerical indicators and descriptive statistics are explained and their importance to quality improvement projects highlighted.

Measuring the central tendency   The central tendency of a set of data refers to the most typical value of that data set. The three measures of central tendency that are most frequently used are the mean, the mode and the median.

Mean

The mean is the arithmetic average of a distribution (or set of data). Often, in practice, the importance and significance of the mean is overrated. Probably it is the most abused statistic in business reporting – and for good reason; it is easy to use and everybody 'understands' it. But it is frequently an unhelpful way to look at data.

A popular example about how misleading the mean can be is that if you had an imaginary patient with their head in an oven and their feet in a freezer then their mean body temperature might be 36°C. Judged by the mean the patient is doing fine. In reality, in order to get a true image of the data questions such as: is the distribution skewed? What is the range? and How dispersed is the data around the mean? also need to be answered.

Six Sigma methods use the full range of statistics when analysing data, to ensure that the accurate situation is determined, analysed and improved.

Median

Another measure of central tendency is the median, which is the number exactly in the middle of the range.

The median is usually a useful indicator of central tendency when the data is ordinal, the distribution is skewed or when we need to filter out outliers (occasional or rare values within our dataset). Figure 3.14 shows the distribution of call duration in an HR Shared Service Centre (HRSSC) of a large oil services company.

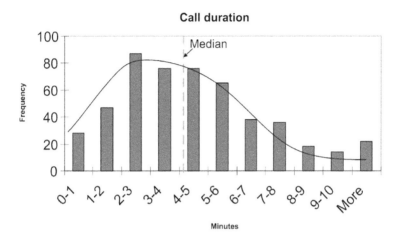

Figure 3.14   Distribution of call duration in an HR shared service centre

This particular distribution meets both criteria that would make an analyst choose the median as a representative measure of central tendency; it is both skewed and there are a number of outliers. On detailed investigation, it might be determined that the outliers highlighted (that is, calls of 11 or more minutes in this example) were actually queries coming from new employees following a small acquisition, which was a one-off event that was not likely to be repeated. Thus, it would not be as accurate to use a central tendency indicator that takes outliers into account, such as the mean, as these are exceptions, not representative for the data set.

Mode

The mode shows the value that is found most frequently in a distribution. Graphically the mode can be easily identified as the highest peak in the histogram.

A distribution can have one major mode and one or more minor or local modes.

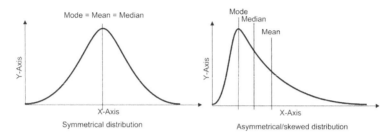

Figure 3.15 Mean, mode and median locations on two different distributions

When to use...

Although each situation is unique and the appropriate method may be different for each case, the choice of measure of central tendency may usually be chosen on the basis of Table 3.4.

Table 3.4 Central tendency measurements for different data types

Data type	Appropriate central tendency measurement	Examples
Nominal	Mode	HR queries by type Trainees by division Hiring costs by role type
Ordinal	Median	Customer satisfaction (rating 1 to 5)
Continuous	Mean	Revenue per employee Cost of hire
Continuous skewed	Median	Time to resolve query Time to hire
Ratio	Mean	HR headcount ratio (HR heads/FTEs to organisational heads/FTEs)
Ratio skewed	Median	Payroll queries per day

Measures of dispersion   Besides range and central tendency, another statistical characteristic of data sets is the dispersion, or how spread or concentrated the data is within its range. Dispersion is also known as variability.

The most common measures of dispersion are variance and standard deviation.

In quality management standard deviation is associated with the unpredictability of the outcomes of processes, the higher the standard deviation, the less predictable the process is, that is why minimising variance as an aim of *Six Sigma* makes perfect sense.

For example, in Figure 3.16 we can see how the difference in the standard deviation of the monthly average of 'cost per hire' for similar roles in two organisations can be clearly observed:

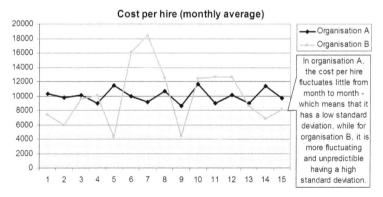

Figure 3.16   Cost per hire example

In this case although both organisations had an average cost per hire of £10,000 for 15 months, the datasets were very different in terms of variance and standard deviation. Therefore in addition to a measure of central tendency, such as the mean or mode, a measure of variation is another important property of datasets that can highlight how fluctuating or unpredictable the values in the set are. The measure of variation provides a view on the stability of the process, something which the mean or mode cannot do. It is the measure that allows you to show how a process that on paper looks as if it delivers the right result is still failing because it is inconsistent.

The measurement plan Based on the team's clear understanding of what type of data can be measured in the process, in order to achieve good results in the measurement phase, a measurement plan must be developed by the team. The measurement plan should include specifications such as:

- the data that is going to be collected;

- sample size for each piece of data;

- operational definitions for each piece of data;

- data collection methods;

- information on who is going to collect the data;

- scheduling the data collection exercise;

- planning how the data is to be used and presented.

The data that needs to be used for analysis might already be available in the corporate management information, HR information systems or customer relationship management systems.

The choice of data collection methods will typically be limited by organisational realities such as which method causes least disruption and which method is most acceptable to those who will be collecting the data so that the maximum reliability of the data is maintained. For example, if the people who are doing a job will also have to measure the effectiveness of their job, they may be tempted to bias measurements in their favour. To instigate this, data should be measured as much as possible through automated means – which is possible with the aid of business applications such as workflow systems and customer relationship management systems, which are commonly used in the service industry. Disturbance within the process caused by measurement usually happens because the measurement tasks themselves affect the output of the overall process.

At the end of the Measure phase, the team will have gathered all the data needed to assess the effectiveness of the current process, and will have done so in a way that minimises the need to gather data which is not relevant or will not be used. Frequently organisations either gather data that is not relevant to the problem they are trying to solve, or gather so much data that little that is effective can be done with it. Running a clear Measurement phase means that real thought will be applied to the data collection, minimising wasteful work but making sure the data needed is in place.

The final stage of the Measure phase is to communicate the result. Communication features at the end of each *Six Sigma* phase, as an indicator that stakeholders must be kept up to date, affected and interested parties and so on. The *Six Sigma* approach itself does not define particular tools and methodologies for this communication, and we suggest you craft a communication and engagement plan for your transformation project that runs for the life of the project, focusing on maintaining high stakeholder engagement throughout.

Case study – Part VII (Measure)

M.3   Data collection plan

In order to collect the requisite data, the *Six Sigma* team used two custom built online (web) applications as follows:

- query data collection tool: This tool was built to collect the data regarding customer queries. For every call the following variables are entered into the query tool:

  - average time to answer (Automatically obtained from phone switch),

  - hand off or not (Yes/No – entered by operator),

  - call duration (measured by switch from the answer to hang up),

  - standardised procedure available (Yes/No – entered by operator),

  - knowledge base needed (Yes/No – entered by operator),

  - if needed – answer found in knowledge base (Yes/No – entered by operator),

  - department,

  - query type,

  - query complexity (1 to 5 rating of complexity),

  - comments.

(In this example the HRSSC did not use any case management tools at the time when the project was undertaken.)

In Figure 3.17, we can see a screenshot of the data collection tool that was used by 15 operators to record key call data. Such a popup would be triggered automatically when the operator closed a call. Time in queue, start and end time were taken automatically from the phone switch.

An obvious effect of using such a tool is that it affects the operators' productivity since they have to perform the extra task of completing this form after each call, however during the pilot test, the team was able to measure that after a few hours of using the tool, the average time needed to fill in the call info form was 3.2 seconds, which is a negligible quantity compared to the average queue waiting time or call duration.

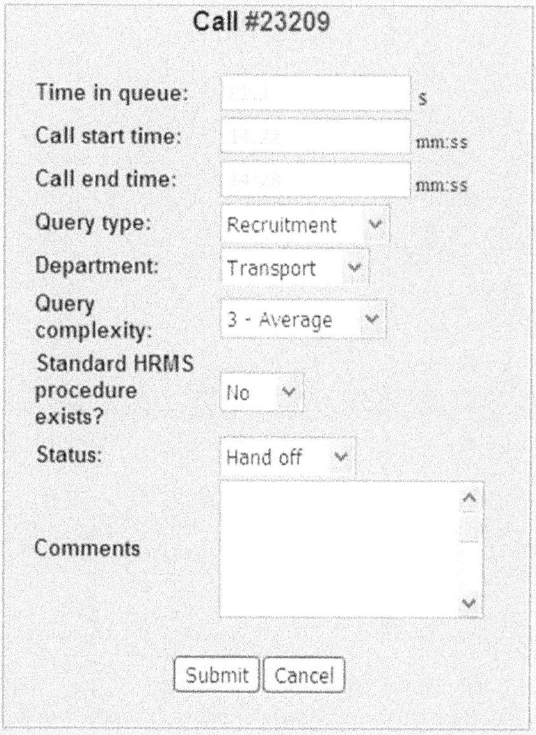

Call #23209

Time in queue:	[____] s
Call start time:	[____] mm:ss
Call end time:	[____] mm:ss
Query type:	Recruitment ∨
Department:	Transport ∨
Query complexity:	3 - Average ∨
Standard HRMS procedure exists?	No ∨
Status:	Hand off ∨
Comments	[_____]

Submit   Cancel

Figure 3.17   Screenshot of a data collection tool

To extend the team's ability to measure non value-added activities, data such as call duration, department and comments have been collected for both inbound and outbound calls. A key difference between an HRSSC and other types of call centres, such as IT support centres, is that in the course of their duties, HRSSC operators often have to make calls and deal with internal or external parties such as line managers, service providers, and so on.

• assessment tool – the assessment tool contains eight questionnaires that have been completed by HRSSC operators and their managers in order to assess their skills. Assessment questionnaires on the following subjects were used:

  – recruitment,

  – performance management,

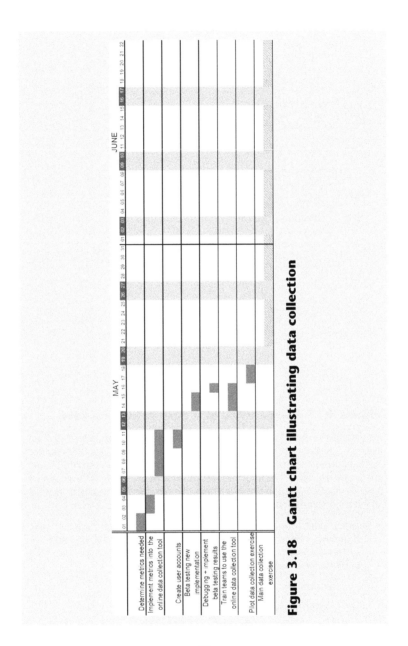

Figure 3.18 Gantt chart illustrating data collection

- training,
- employee relations,
- payroll and benefits,
- pensions and leavers,
- HRMS (HR management system knowledge/skills),
- a general assessment (contains general and customer relations assessment).

Besides the above data collected using online data collection applications, the team also collected the following indicators:

- general daily metrics. For each day of functioning of the HRSSC, the *Six Sigma* team also collected or computed the following variables:
  - absenteeism (per cent of HRSSC employees on leave),
  - total number of calls/day (calculated from the data collected through the collection tool).

The query data collection exercise was scheduled to take place, according to Figure 3.18 opposite, between the 1st of May and 22nd of June.

Brief information about the query data collection activity:

- total number of operators in the HRSSC: 20;
- operators taking part in data collection: 15;
- number of days for collecting data: 25;
- estimated average calls per operator per day: 40;
- estimated calls that will be used in data collection: 15,000 (=40*25*15).

ANALYSE

Raw data which has not been processed or understood is of little to no value for anyone. The key to getting value out of data is always through analysis. It is said that highly skilled alchemists of the past were in possession of tools and techniques that allowed them to transform common metals into gold.

By applying quantitative and qualitative information analysis methods *Six Sigma* teams can transform raw, apparently random data into intelligence that is of significant value to organisations that they work for. For the HR *Six Sigma* project, a strong piece of analysis can make the difference between being a successful HR change project and failure.

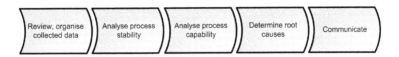

Figure 3.19   Sample analyse phase steps

ANALYSE PROCESS PERFORMANCE OVER TIME

The achievement of operational excellence in most HR operations requires the achievement of consistency of process outputs. Customers do not perceive averages, what they perceive when purchasing goods or services are actually the variances – the difference between their expectations and the quality of the service actually delivered. In reality all processes and activities will have natural variations and absolute consistency is not a realistic goal. This is because processes have a natural variance based on a large number of small, random, unknown factors that cause fluctuations in process outputs and which result in a steady distribution around the average data point. The fact that these variations are caused by unknown factors also means that these causes are beyond our control and exist within the process naturally. This type of variation is also known as 'noise' by *Six Sigma* teams.

Since process outputs are affected by many types of internal and external events, often some of these events do not constitute common sources of variation – they are not small, nor are they random – yet they can still have a considerable impact on the overall variation of the process thus spoiling plans of a lean, mean, low variance process. Luckily, these secondary sources of variation are known factors or factors that can be discovered and therefore can often be controlled or eliminated completely. These are called special causes of variation and cause process output variations due to specific factors that must be identified and removed as a measure of quality management. The special causes of variation are the focus of *Six Sigma* teams, as eliminating them is the only way of getting the process under control.

The overall variation of any process aggregates both common and special cause variations.

Imagine the River Thames that flows through London, the small waves on its surface caused by the flow of water, the small random movement of air currents and the configuration of the bottom of the river give the natural variance to the river's surface – these waves are many, small, random and very hard to predict at a low level. However, when a ship passes by, it generates a separate type of wave that add to the general movement or variation of the water surface. The ship's movement in this case is a known, large, predictable cause of variation, thus a special cause.

Similarly in an HRSSC team small day-to-day differences in the number of queries can occur due to a large number of random factors. But if the payroll function is malfunctioning it can generate a wave of queries at the beginning of the month that aggregate into the overall variance of the variable just like the ship passing through the river. In this case the low performance of the payroll processes is a special cause that can be identified and improvements worked on by a *Six*

Sigma team. In reality, however, we usually have more than one special cause of variation which makes identifying them more difficult.

The purpose of the Analyse phase is to take the measured data and identify variations and their causes. These can then be investigated and changed in the Improve phase to create a better process that supports excellence in HR service delivery.

RUN CHARTS

Run charts are time series plots that display how the process performs over time. They are usually a part of preliminary analyses and are used to:

- spot patterns in data that suggest trends;

- analyse types and sources of variation;

- monitor and control performance;

- communicate findings.

In the HR context, run charts can be used to study a large number of process outputs (Ys), both in the HR operations and people management areas such as: number of queries solved within SLA, time to fill vacancies, and so on.

In a run chart, the output variable of the process is plotted on the y axis, against time on the x axis.

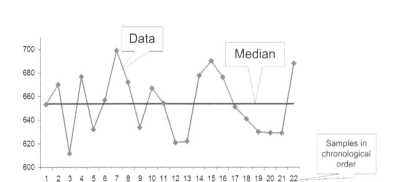

Figure 3.20   Anatomy of a run chart

Interpreting run charts

There are three main types of patterns to look for when interpreting a run chart. These are: runs, trends and cycles.

For a run chart with 25 data points, these patterns would be interpreted as follows (see Figure 3.21):

- runs – any series of eight consecutive points that are not on the median or in its close proximity. It does not matter whether they are increasing or decreasing in value – the fact that all points are on the same side of a median qualifies this pattern as a run. Whenever a *Six Sigma* team have such

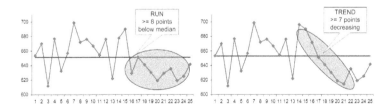

Figure 3.21   Runs and trends

a sequence of points on either side of the median, they will investigate to find what special cause created this anomaly;

- trends – any sequence of seven or more consecutive points increasing or decreasing in value. Such a pattern is often a signal that there is an underlying special cause affecting the outputs of the process;

- cycles – any other pattern that recurs eight times or more in a row.

The motivation that stands behind pattern interpretation of run charts is of a probabilistic nature. For example if we toss a coin 25 times there is an extremely low probability that it will show either heads or tails eight times consecutively. However if this does happen we can suspect that there is an external factor which caused this anomaly, like the person tossing the coin cheating in some way. This is a special cause of variation that ideally must be eliminated. In a similar way, the probability of a process outcome to fall eight times out of 25 on one side of the median, under common conditions (natural variation) is so small that a special cause should be suspected and investigated. The probability of having a run of five under common conditions is much higher so, the longer the pattern, the higher the probability that there is a special cause of variation.

The length of these patterns is not fixed at eight of course and the length analysed should be chosen in each case depending on the impact that eliminating a potentially existing special cause would have on the process performance. There are times when the process is so important that even if the chance of having a special cause is small then a *Six Sigma* team should still investigate.

As these kinds of interpretations are based on probabilities, there is also the probability that there are erroneous signals, or that the pattern occurred naturally without any special cause. However, experience suggests that in most cases, if the data set is large enough then finding these patterns is a clear sign worthy of full investigation.

CONTROL CHARTS

Control charts are a specialised type of run charts. During the 1920s, Bell Labs were one of the first organisations to use control charts as a means to identify special causes of variation in the manufacturing process of telephony equipment. Bell Labs demonstrated that there were significant financial benefits to bringing production processes under statistical control by having only common cause variation.

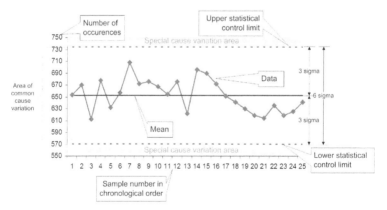

Figure 3.22   Anatomy of a control chart

Basically control charts can be interpreted by looking at the control limits (which are set at +/- 3 standard deviations around the mean); if there are any points outside these, then this is a sign that the process outcome is affected by a special cause. However, more complex sets of rules for control chart interpretation have been developed such as the Nelson rules shown in the table below.

Table 3.5   The   Nelson   rules   for   control   chart interpretation

Rule	Chart pattern	Interpretation
1	One point is more than 3 standard deviations from the mean *on either side (within the special cause variation area).*	*One sample is grossly out of control.*
2	Nine (or more) points in a row are on the same side of the mean.	*Some prolonged bias exists.*
3	Six (or more) points in a row are continually increasing (or decreasing).	*A trend exists. This is directional and the position of the mean and size of the standard deviation do not affect this rule.*
4	Fourteen (or more) points in a row alternate in direction, increasing then decreasing.	*This much oscillation is beyond normal noise. This is directional and the position of the mean and size of the standard deviation do not affect this rule.*
5	Two (or three) out of three points in a row are more than 2 standard deviations from the mean in the same direction.	*There is a medium tendency for samples to be out of control.*
6	Four out of five points in a row are more than 1 standard deviation from the mean in the same direction.	*There is a strong tendency for samples to be slightly out of control.*
7	Fifteen points in a row are all within 1 standard deviation of the mean on either side of the mean.	*With 1 standard deviation, greater variation would be expected.*
8	Eight points in a row exist with none within 1 standard deviation of the mean and the points are in both directions from the mean.	*Jumping from above to below whilst missing the first standard deviation band is rarely random.*

Similar probability thinking as used with run charts is valid for the interpretations of control charts; each signal shows that there is a probability of the process being out of statistical control. For example there is a 0.27 per cent probability of having a point outside the 3-sigma control limits. Thus, if a data set has a point outside of the 3-sigma control (that is more than 3 standard deviations away from the mean) then this is a clear indication that something has gone wrong.

However, before trying to improve the performance of a process, *Six Sigma* teams will first make sure that the process is in statistical control, that its behaviour is not chaotic and that they know what to expect from the process when it is operating at expected performance levels. For an HR project where the reason for the change could be that the process is not in statistical control, this can be a challenge. In this instance, the focus in the Analyse phase should be on identifying those things that cause the majority of issues, not focusing on the outliers. This will allow the team to spend their time fixing the real issues.

PROCESS CAPABILITY

Once a process is in statistical control and its outputs are consistent, capability assessment tools can be used to study the process outputs against the required specifications.

A 'capable' process is one whose outputs fall within the specification limits.

Capability analyses contain two main parts:

1. The capability histogram – which shows the distribution of the outputs of the process, the upper and lower specifications limits and usually the best fit distribution.

2. The capability indices – which are numerical values that estimate the capability of the process in respect to the upper and lower limits.

Interpreting capability

Process capability is a measure of how well a process that is in control performs within its specification limits. The capability can be measured using capability ratios or indices such as Cp or Cpk.

$$Cp = \frac{Specified\ variation}{Real\ variation\ of\ the\ process} = \frac{Upper\_Specification\_Limit - Lower\_Specification\_Limit}{6\sigma}$$

Cp is a ratio of the allowed variation of the process (variation within technical specifications) and its real variation. This shows how close the variation of the process is to the desired variation.

Cpk is an index of how close the process is delivering within the specification limits taking into account its natural variance. Cpk calculates the upper variance (above the target) and lower variance (below the target) separately, which is useful when the distribution or specification limits are not symmetrical. The larger the Cpk, the fewer the number of occurrences outside the specification limits.

Figure 3.23 can be used as an example to illustrate the difference between Cp and Cpk. Suppose that a hunter is training to shoot arrows and most of them hit the target close to one another forming a cluster. In this case the shooting process has a high Cp ratio, regardless of how close or far the cluster is from the bullseye. However if the Cpk is high too, then the cluster formed is on, or very close to, the bullseye.

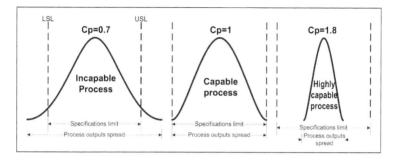

Figure 3.23   The examples of process capability (Cp)

In the charts above we can see three situations that process capability (Cp) can show:

- Cp<1 – the process produces outputs outside the specification limits – the lower the Cp value, the more outputs fall out of the specification limits;

- Cp=1 – the process outputs are exactly within the specification limits – meaning that sometimes the output is equal (or extremely close) to one of the specification limits. Although this is considered a capable process, at the slightest drift the outputs will fall outside of the specification limits;

- Cp>1 – all process outputs fall within the specification and there is a gap between the highest and lowest output and upper and lower specification limits respectively. In this case, even in the case of a drift there is enough space to keep the outputs within the specification limits.

When the capability is calculated longer term, different types of ratios and indices are used called process performance indices (and noted with Pp and Ppk). The difference in calculating process performance is in the way normal variation is computed.

Since these ratios are unitless they can be used to compare the capabilities of different processes for benchmark purposes.

The importance of these indices is very high for *Six Sigma* teams because they offer clear quantitative measurements of process capability/performance which can be used as benchmarks when simulating, pilot testing or implementing improvements to the process.

Usually during this part of the methodology, statistical skills are needed to choose the most appropriate analysis methods depending on the data types being analysed and project objectives. In the HR Shared Services project used as a case study, the team analysed the call duration data using the *Six Sigma* specialised software package Minitab. In this case a test was firstly performed to determine whether the distribution of data was normal or not. This in turn helped the team in plotting and computing process capability.

Case study – Part VIII (Analyse)

A.1 Analysis of call duration data

As seen in the following normality test (Andersen-Darling), the distribution of call duration is far from being normal. (Graphically, the more dots lie along the line the better the distribution resembles normal distribution. In this case very few dots are on the line).

However this is not uncommon when measuring lifetimes of 'objects'[1,2] where often the best fit distribution is Weibull (a probability distribution that can model many natural phenomena when the data is normally distributed or even if it is not – as in this case). This is one of the many examples in *Six Sigma* when data is proven not to be normally distributed (its distribution is not bell shaped – nor Gaussian).

In order to calculate the process capability or performance indices correctly, the type of distribution needs to be taken into account (see Figure 3.25).

---

1   Woflram Mathworld – 'Weibull Distribution' – mathworld.wolfram.com.
2   Wikipedia – 'Weibull' – *'Weibull [...] may be used to represent [...] delivery times'.*

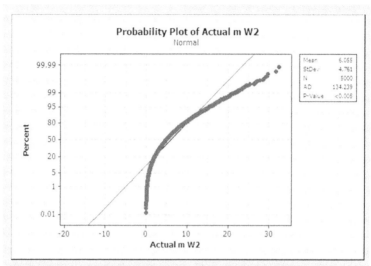

Figure 3.24 Testing the normal distribution fit of call duration

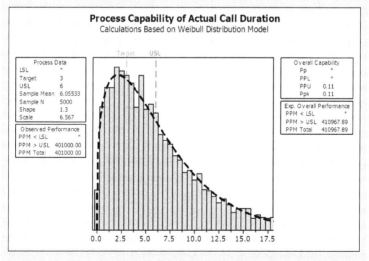

Figure 3.25 Process capability of actual call duration

In the chart we can see that the processes' performance is very low (Ppk = 0.11) having 410,967 defects per million. However, the process is stable as indicated by the Xbar chart of actual call duration.

The target call duration level for the current HRSSC was set to 3 minutes with a maximum acceptable level of 6 minutes, however in almost half of the cases the duration was way above this boundary. The maximum acceptable level or Upper Specification Limit (USL) sets a boundary within which the duration can fluctuate (usually due to its natural variance). This boundary is used to compute the process capability indices which can be used to measure the improvement or benchmark.

ROOT CAUSES

The following section outlines a number of creative analysis tools that can be used to determine the root causes of a problem you are trying to transform. These tools can be used to deliver additional insight into the situation and to the possible solutions.

THE MODEL

In addition to statistical analysis, the Analyse phase includes many very helpful interpretative tools for the HR improvement project. These tools give a structure and rigour to improvement suggestions, a valuable thing in being able to talk to the business about what change will be made and why. A simple creativity enhancing model that can drive process improvement is called THE. This groups improvement suggestions into the following three categories:

1. **T**echnology driven improvements.

2. **H**uman elements where different behaviours or team interactions could help.

3. Environment (internal and external) covering issues linked to organisational policies, procedures, suppliers, customers and so on.

This model is helpful because:

- it is simple and straightforward – thus, it can be easily applied to almost any type of group;

- it takes less time to complete than other models like fishbone diagrams;

- it helps avoid duplication of ideas;

- it focuses on the three most important areas of process improvement.

Generally this model can be used in lean or *Six Sigma* workshops aimed at improving high level processes and can generate a few important points that the *Six Sigma* team can focus on.

Table 3.6 is a general example of the type of ideas that can be gathered using this tool.

ISHIKAWA (FISHBONE DIAGRAMS) AND 5 WHYS

An Ishikawa diagram, also known as fishbone or cause and effect diagram is a powerful tool that can help *Six Sigma* teams dig into the causes and sub-causes of defects in processes.

The creator of this model, Kaoru Ishikawa, created the model with six main categories, known as the 6Ms; Machine, Method, Materials, Measurement, Man and Mother Nature.

Table 3.6   Using 3 basic areas of process improvement – technology, human and environment

Problem: Improving HR service delivery		
Potential solutions		
Technology	**Human**	**Environment**
• Implement a full knowledge base on HR issues • Leverage self-service • Make interfaces more user-friendly/ efficient to use • One point of entry for any data piece • One centralised database – one version of the truth • Improve network slowdown issues	• Make sure the employees in HR are better connected to the realities of the business • Improve the relationships between HRBPs and line managers • Train managers to use the self-service better	• Ensure better communications within the organisation (of changes, processes, policies, and so on) • Increase the perception of HR's strategic importance in the organisation • Strengthen relationships with suppliers (technology, services, and so on)

However, there are situations, especially in HR services, where other categories would be more appropriate. These typically are: Equipment, Process, People, Materials, Environment and Management, or a simpler set called 4Ss which covers Surroundings, Suppliers, Systems and Skills.

To get to the real root causes the teams must dig as deep as possible. The 5Ws method can be used for such an approach. 5Ws means asking "why?" five times in order to get to the deeper causes, for example:

It takes a long time for HR queries to the Service Centre to be resolved.

• why? – service agents are too slow to provide information;

- why? – they don't always have the necessary information to hand;

- why? – information is located in different places within the organisation;

- why? – there is no central database;

- why? – there is no consistent organisation-wide technology strategy.

Of course, asking why five times does get a little frustrating for people who participate in these exercises so it needs to be used sparingly.

Another pitfall of the 5Ws is that it only takes into account one branch of what could be a whole tree structure of root causes. Using the Ishikawa diagram and 5Ws together will reveal most root causes of HR service problems and help prioritise areas for further investigations and improvements.

Good results typically come from using these tools in workshops with groups of four to 12 people with understanding of how a process operates and who can generate insights into the working of the process that would otherwise be missed by the *Six Sigma* team.

The causes for low customer satisfaction identified throughout the case study project were broken down into categories and mapped on a fishbone diagram as seen in the following section.

Method 1 – using predefined categories

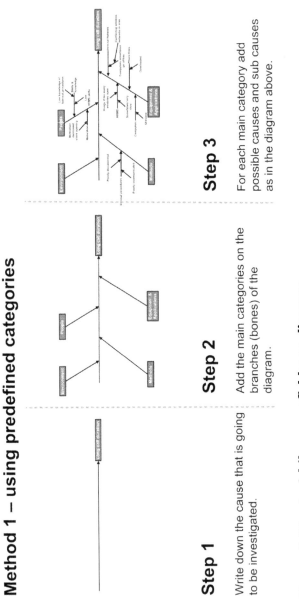

Step 1

Write down the cause that is going to be investigated.

Step 2

Add the main categories on the branches (bones) of the diagram.

Step 3

For each main category add possible causes and sub causes as in the diagram above.

Figure 3.26 An Ishikawa or fishbone diagram

Method 2 – clustering

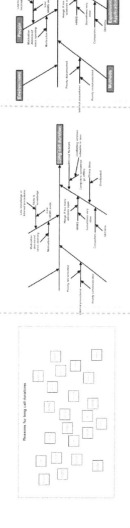

Step 1

Write down all the reasons why the problem might occur. (Brainstorming or nominal group technique – using post it notes)

Step 2

Cluster the causes detected into groups and sub-groups around the branches of the diagram.

Step 3

Name the clusters that have been formed.

Figure 3.27 Clustering

Case study example – Part IX (Analyse)

A.2 Cause and effect analysis

Following the detailed measurements, assessments and focus group organised during the measurement phase, the team was able to identify the most important causes that lead to longer call durations, lowering customer satisfaction.

Figure 3.28 shows a typical set of internal issues that are causing interference to effective HR service delivery in an organisation.

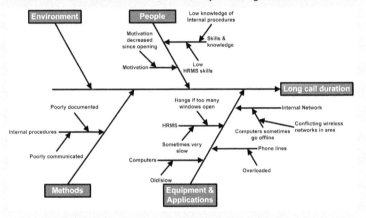

Figure 3.28 Fishbone diagram illustrating obstacles to effective HR service delivery

ANALYSIS OF VARIANCE (ANOVA)

Ishikawa and THE models provide a helpful means for *Six Sigma* teams to generate hypotheses as to why certain defects are occurring. In business process improvement work, to detect problems and find solutions, different hypotheses have to be made. Is the process performance affected by the location of employees? Is it affected by their training level? Different technological issues? Weather? And so on. Often the hypotheses might sound sensible and make sense. But are they really valid?

To answer this question, statistics provide a set of methods which by analysing the variance within a process can prove whether or not its output is affected by one or more causes proposed in the hypotheses.

The sets of methods that enable the running of these statistical analyses are known as ANOVA which stands for 'ANalysis Of VAriance'. These methods are very popular not just with *Six Sigma* experts but also with scientists and in particular with psychologists and medical researchers who use them to study the efficiency of newly developed medicines or the causes of illnesses. Almost all medicines on the market are there because they have passed one type or another of ANOVA testing. Similarly *Six Sigma* teams can use them to study the causes of defects or even the efficiency of different suggested improvements.

The subject of analysis of variance is vast and ranges from proving simple hypotheses such as whether or not an effect is caused by one or more causes, to more complex situations when hypothesis testing is needed for multiple effects (dependent variables) simultaneously, in which case it is called multivariate analysis of variance. Luckily in most *Six Sigma* projects just the simplest types of ANOVA are needed, which can be computed using the 'Data analysis pack' provided with Microsoft Excel. Therefore we will focus on one simple example of hypothesis testing for *Six Sigma* using ANOVA.

Generally, ANOVA can be used when the variance of a continuous variable such as cost is suspected to be influenced by different identifiable causes. Some examples of hypotheses that can be tested using ANOVA in HR could be:

- the HRSSC query duration is influenced by query type;

- the query duration depends on the administration employee's self-assessment scores;

- the time to fill a job is influenced by site location.

Even though some of these might make sense at first sight, are they always real facts? And if so what's the probability they aren't valid?

In reality such hypotheses are not always valid, their validity varying from process to process, organisation to organisation, country to country and so on. Therefore once hypotheses have been formulated, it's best to test their validity using data collected during the measurement phase and to discover those causes that really make a difference in the performance of the process.

Perhaps the following example will help explain even further the importance of ANOVA. A new supposedly more efficient user interface was developed for a Shared Services Centre's HR management system. The initial hypothesis is that the new interface will reduce the cost of queries. To prove whether this hypothesis holds true or not, the *Six Sigma* team started a pilot test by gathering data and computing the cost for 100 queries handled by two Shared Services employees who used the new interface. In parallel the cost of 100 queries dealt with using the old interface was calculated.

We have frequently seen that the data in each group can at first glance look very similar. The range of query times might be very similar and the average or mean query handling duration might be near identical. But when analysed in more detail, the data for each day might have quite different highs, lows or variances. Even if the means are different, this is not enough difference to draw any conclusion yet. In this example, ANOVA was applied to the data around a continuous variable (cost per transaction) split in to two groups; transactions processed through the new interface and transactions processed through the old interface.

In this case our hypotheses would be formulated formally as:

H_0 – the type of user interface (old or new) does not influence the query clearance cost;

H_1 – the type of user interface does influence the query clearance cost.

ANOVA performed for two groups of data returns a set of results as shown in Figure 3.29.

ANOVA: Single Factor

SUMMARY

Groups	Count	Sum	Average	Variance	
Old interface	100	855.7828	8.557828	15.76089	1 – Dataset summary
New interface	100	727.8914	7.278914	3.940222	

2 – Computing parameters   3- Interpretation results

ANOVA

Source of Variation	SS	df	MS	F	P-value	F crit
Between Groups	81.78104	1	81.78104	8.302176	0.004396	3.888853
Within Groups	1950.41	198	9.850555			
Total	2032.191	199				

Figure 3.29   ANOVA analysis of two sets of data

We can split these results in to three main categories:

1. Dataset summary – presents summary statistics about the data.

2. Computing parameters – parameters used in computing the F ratio (see below).

3. Interpretation results – the essential part of ANOVA that is used in interpreting the results and drawing conclusions.

The results used for interpretation consist of the following three values:

F: the F ratio represents the ratio of the two independent estimations of variance.

P-value: the probability that the result happened purely by chance.

F-critical: can be considered the benchmark that the F ratio of the groups must be compared with to accept or reject the initial hypothesis.

The analysis uses a statistical hypothesis testing method called F-test which is interpreted by comparing F ratio to F critical. The basic rule of interpretation of this analysis is that if F >= F critical, then reject H_0 otherwise accept H_0 as true.

In the ANOVA results shown above the F ratio is greater than F critical, therefore we reject H_0, meaning that the type of interface used does influence the query clearance cost – which confirms our initial hypothesis. As the P-value is a measure of the probability that the difference between these two sets happened just by chance or how significant the conclusion is. Here it implies that the likelihood of the hypothesis being true is down to chance is 0.4 per cent – that is, it's not very likely. Similarly there is a 99.4 per cent chance that the interface used does influence the cost of query clearance.

The significance of the result is one of the most important outputs of ANOVA. Simply comparing the mean values of datasets gives no view on how significant the difference between them is. Only by analysing the variance can we get a clear view of how significantly different two groups of data are (or not).

PARETO ANALYSIS

In order to effectively manage project outcomes and to focus energy where it will have the greatest impact, it is critical to understand the relative importance of the issues affecting the quality of the HR Service. The Pareto principle, also known as the 80/20 rule or the law of the vital few, states that for many events 80 per cent of the effects come from 20 per cent of the causes. Applied to process improvement this would mean that 80 per cent of defects come from 20 per cent of defect causes.

Pareto charts are bar charts where the values are arranged in decreasing order, to show the importance of different causes and whether or not the Pareto principle applies. On the Y axis the frequency is shown and on the X axis, the categories that our data is split by, as seen in Figure 3.30.

The cumulative (black) line shows how many of the effects happen because of the causes up to that point in the chart. For example, in the second chart, the line intersects the 50 per cent horizontal border at the third bar which means that 50 per cent of the outgoing calls are either to HRMS support, training suppliers or internal.

In *Six Sigma* projects Pareto charts can be used when there is a need to determine the relative importance of elements such as:

- different projects that are proposed to sponsors for them to confirm priorities (Project selection);

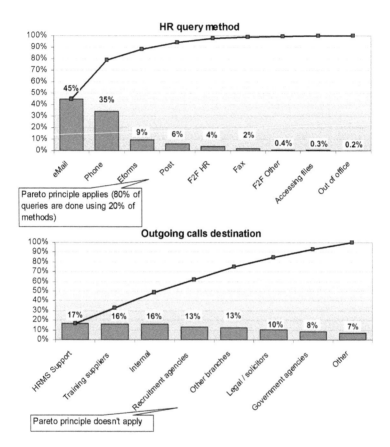

Figure 3.30   Using the Pareto principle

- different characteristics for customers (Define);

- relative importance of different metrics that are being considered for use (Measure);

- the key factors affecting the quality of a product or service (Analyse);

- selecting the best alternatives for process improvement (Improve).

The Pareto analysis can also identify whether the Pareto 80/20 rule applies in a situation. Whilst there are a number of instances when the belief that 80 per cent of defects come from 20 per cent of causes will hold true it cannot be assumed to be a cast-iron rule. In reality the Pareto principle may not apply and the *Six Sigma* team will need to show whether it is relevant or not by hard analysis.

In a process improvement project, when the Pareto principle applies to the causes of defects, it gives an indication of what the main areas that need attention are. When Pareto does not apply it is an indication that another dimension may need to be explored to identify issues.

For example, if there are ten main causes for defects and no Pareto effect, then the team could use the cost needed to eliminate each cause as a third dimension, and add it as a weight to the chart to produce a new, weighted Pareto chart that can aid the decision process much better by showing the cheapest solution that will have the biggest impact.

CAUSAL LOOP DIAGRAMS

The tools mentioned so far miss out one important element, consideration of the links between the inputs and outputs of a process and how these impact the defects that occur. A useful yet little known tool in the analysis phase is the Causal Loop Diagram (CLD). This has its origins in system dynamics as a method to develop understanding of complex systems. It shows how inputs (Xs) and outputs (Ys) are interlinked in a system to produce a chain of causes and effects.

The tool is simple to use. It consists of variables and arrows that connect these variables showing how they interact with one another (the correlation between them being shown by either a plus or minus sign). Basically the correlation sign means that for plus, when the value of the cause variable rises, so does the value of the effect variable (for example, if query duration rises, cost rises). Obviously if a negative correlation exists, it is shown by the minus sign (for example, if query duration rises, customer satisfaction decreases).

As its name suggests, besides the cascading causes that the diagram brings into the light, it also uncovers loops within the system. These loops can be either reinforcing or balancing. Reinforcing loops consist of those chains of casual relationships

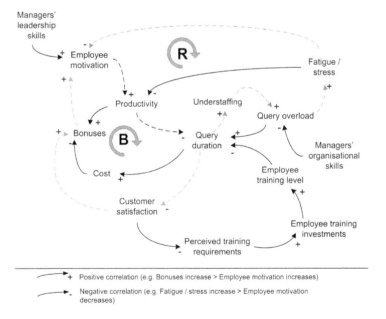

Figure 3.31   A causal loop diagram

that loop creating exponential growth of variables' values or collapsing them. This type of loop needs special attention since they can, under certain conditions, lead to the collapse of the system as a whole.

The example in Figure 3.32, related to the main case study, focuses on the query duration, and aims to show the cascading and looping chains of causes and effects that are directly or indirectly linked to it. This diagram is valid just for the case study presented, as the chains of causes and effects can differ from organisation to organisation.

The reinforcing loop identified shows a common symptom of overloading in service industries (generally overloading causes stress that reduces productivity that in turn causes more overloading, in this particular case leading to higher query duration and ultimately lower customer satisfaction). This loop often acts as a trap for service organisations and if not balanced by other elements can lead to the collapse of the service delivery processes.

An example of a balancing loop, in this case, is the cascade of causes and effects between query duration – customer satisfaction – employee motivation and productivity. In this case bonuses are given on a yearly base following customer satisfaction surveys run by the company. The simultaneous existence of more reinforcing and balancing loops in a system can keep the system in balance. However detecting imbalances early on can help improve the system and reduce the variation of its outputs.

In analysing the causal loops discovered in the diagram, the team should take into account the cycle time of each loop (the time it takes for the effects to be produced by a chain of causes and

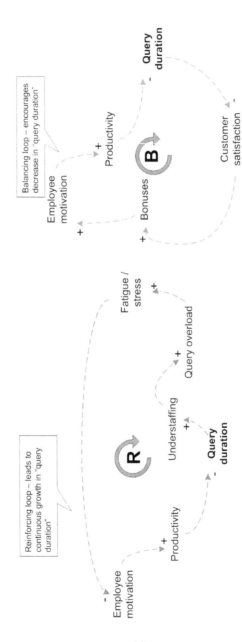

Figure 3.32 A reinforcing and a balancing loop

effects). In this case the balancing loop has a much higher cycle time (months, quarters) than the reinforcing whose cycle time could be a matter of a day. This difference in cycle times increases the danger that the reinforcing loop poses to the process.

Besides cycle times and correlations, in reality each of these variables also has a probability distribution (mean and standard deviation). Transforming this diagram into a mathematical model and including data collected during measurements can enable us to perform different types of Monte Carlo simulations to test possible improvement scenarios without the risk of having the process fail in reality (see page 95 for more on Monte Carlo simulations).

At the end of the Analyse phase the team has not only gathered data relevant to the process, but more importantly has spent significant time using both quantitative and qualitative methods to interpret the meaning of the data. For HR transformation project teams, working through a selection of the tools described above provides a robust conclusion as to what to change and why which can be used to make sure the business understands and accepts the need for the change before going on to start the Transformation itself. All too frequently HR functions find themselves part way through a change being asked why it is happening. A clear piece of analysis work, data driven as well as interpretative, will help to avoid this scenario, or at least to provide clear answers to questions which challenge the project.

IMPROVE

One of the great advantages of the *Six Sigma* process for HR Transformation is the time and thought it imposes on understanding the issues before jumping to a solution. But once the issues are understood, the rigour of *Six Sigma* can equally be applied to the change process itself. So far the focus has been on collecting data, analysing the current situation and transforming raw data into valuable intelligence. Attention now turns to thinking about improving the process so that it is redesigned to be capable, predictable and able to fully meet customer requirements.

Sample improvement phase steps

Figure 3.33   Sample improvement phase steps

The analysis completed prior to this stage may indicate that the process is so badly performing that a wholescale redesign is required. In such a case, the team would apply DMADV methodology instead of DMAIC, to design and verify a new process instead of improving and controlling the current one. However, in most cases a few improvement actions will be enough and the team will normally adopt the DMAIC route.

During the Improve phase, the need for creativity is probably at a premium in the *Six Sigma* project so that the status quo can be challenged and tested by new ideas.

Managing change is also a key element of the Improve phase, since any improvement means doing something differently. The *Six Sigma* team will need to make recommendations for what to change in the process, how to alter the way people complete tasks and suggestions on how to change the technology used. Sometimes the changes recommended and implemented are subtle and unnoticeable to the people involved in the delivery of the process. But, most often the changes proposed will be significant and have a major impact on the staff and customers involved. Change management strategies will need to be developed to manage these issues and the impact on the business of any new proposals.

As expected with any *Six Sigma* phase, a strong empirical, mathematical component also exists during the Improve phase – since the team must test and prove empirically that the improvements recommended will have a positive impact on the predictability and capability of the process. Usually pilot studies are organised, rolled out and analysed to test the proposed improvements in a real environment.

GENERATING POTENTIAL SOLUTIONS

To generate potential solutions the team can use tools that encourage 'out of the box' thinking and the generation of new ideas. Such tools include brainstorming, nominal group technique, visualisation and Six Thinking Hats.

Nominal group technique is a solution generating method that involves 'silent generation of ideas' – instead of an open flow of ideas like in brainstorming, when using the nominal group technique, the participants write down their ideas silently on pieces of paper, which are then discussed and analysed by the group. It is more useful than brainstorming for those groups that have members who are reluctant to communicate their ideas directly or create debate.

Past experiences, best practice case studies or external expertise are just a few examples of sources for improvement ideas that *Six Sigma* teams should look into.

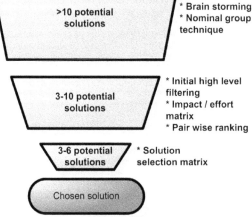

Sample solution filtering pipeline

Figure 3.34   Solution generation

SELECTING AND PRIORITISING

Once the shortlist of three to six potential solutions are ready, a criterion ranking matrix can be used to select the most appropriate solution by taking into account the importance of critical characteristics and how each of these solutions scores for them.

Figure 3.35 shows an example of how such a matrix was used to prioritise *Six Sigma* processes within a construction company.

This criterion matrix that shows the ranking of potential projects was developed and used as follows:

- the *Six Sigma* team identified the criteria list and assigned weights according to their importance to the organisation

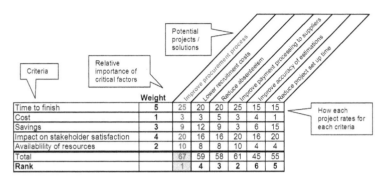

Criteria	Weight	Improve procurement process	Lower recruitment costs	Reduce absenteeism	Improve payment processing to suppliers	Improve accuracy of estimations	Reduce project set up time
Time to finish	5	25	20	20	25	15	15
Cost	1	3	3	5	3	4	1
Savings	3	9	12	9	3	6	15
Impact on stakeholder satisfaction	4	20	16	16	20	16	20
Availablility of resources	2	10	8	8	10	4	4
Total		67	59	58	61	45	55
Rank		1	4	3	2	6	5

Figure 3.35   Six Sigma processes in a construction company

together with four stakeholders, prior to organising the workshop;

- during the interactive workshop, the participants completed the ratings in each project-to-criteria cell;

- the scores were then summed up to produce a prioritisation list for each project.

In practice, if the ratings are agreed upon during a workshop, it is advisable to hide the weights at the beginning and only use them after the whole matrix has been completed so that prior knowledge of the weighting does not bias the respondents' ratings.

SIMULATIONS AND PILOT STUDIES

Once a viable solution has been identified it is wise to pilot test the improved or redesigned process before rolling it out across the business. Testing the process can be done through simulations and pilot studies.

The main aims of running pilot tests are to:

- understand the variation within the new process;

- find further improvements;

- mitigate risks;

- confirm assumptions and improve the business case;

- assess the true performance in a live environment.

Simulations are generally constructed as mathematical models that try to mimic the behaviour of the real environment and produce results or Ys as probability distributions. The main advantage of running simulations is that a number of different scenarios can be tested relatively quickly and with minimum costs and risks.

Some of the most widely used simulation methods are the Monte Carlo simulations which are methods of approximating the value of a function (Y or process output) by performing very large numbers of trials based on real probability distributions of input variables. As these methods take into account probabilities, the results will also have probabilities assigned.

For example, given the inputs and mathematical model of the improved query management process, the Monte Carlo method can return as one of the results the potential probability distribution of 'call clearance time', where the probability that the process will be within the service level agreement can be studied.

Until recently the use of Monte Carlo methods was reserved to a privileged few, usually scientists who had access to high-end computer systems and programming resources. Today there are a number of commercial solutions on the market (such as @Risk, Risksolver or Riskamp) that can be used even on low-end personal computers to perform simulations on customised mathematical models.

Pilot studies should be organised with clear objectives and performance assessment systems in place in order to detect and measure improvements achieved and to document the behaviour of the new process.

FORCE FIELD ANALYSIS

While a simulation or pilot study will help assess if the changes to the process have worked, a broader assessment is needed on what else may have to change for the improvement to last. Force field analysis is a method, developed by Kurt Lewin and inspired from mechanical engineering, used for identifying and assessing the drivers and barriers to achieving a particular goal or change.

The tool is simple to use and the analysis can be done in five easy steps:

1. Define the change that is to be implemented – process improvements.

2. List on one side of the central line the drivers for change and on the other side the barriers to the change.

3. Assign a weight to each of the forces – estimating how powerful it is.

4. Calculate the sums of weights on each side to see which is more powerful.

5. Determine action plans.

Once there is a clear image of what the driving and restraining forces for change are, the team can act to reinforce the driving ones while reducing or even eliminating the restraints. Like most other tools presented, this tool achieves its best results if applied during a workshop and combined with facilitated techniques such as brain storming or nominal group technique. Workshop participants can come with ideas as to what the driving and restraining forces are, assign weights either by voting or averaging, and brain storm to generate action plans.

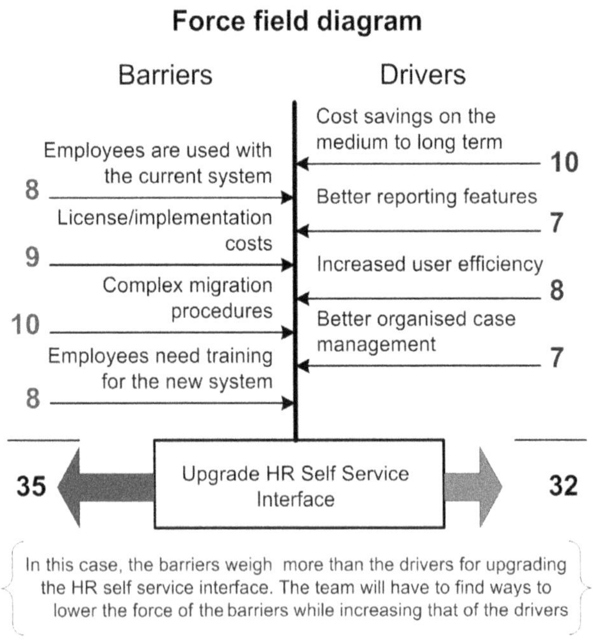

Force field diagram

Figure 3.36 Force field analysis

Solutions that can improve the performance of the process and reduce the number of defects are the desired outcomes of the improve phase. The list of solutions shortlisted in the HRSSC case study are listed in the following section.

Once you have identified the solutions, these can be implemented in whatever way is appropriate. *Six Sigma* does not go in to the means you will use to implement the solution, precisely because there is an infinite number of potential problems being investigated and therefore solutions to them. You may find you are now embarking on a substantial technology change project, or a restructure. Or you may be re-working a critical step in a recruitment process. Each of these implementations will require a different type of focus. The next stage at which you will enter the *Six Sigma* methodology is once you have made the change, where the tools to keep your process in Control come in to play.

Case study example – Part X (Improve)

I.1   Improving the HRSSC call clearance process

Given the causes identified during analysis, the team found a number of areas that if acted upon would have the highest impact on improving the process and ultimately employee satisfaction. After filtering out over 15 potential solutions, the following three have been chosen to be implemented as having the best cost to impact ratio:

I.1.1 Immediate improvements:

1.   People

Problem: low skills in working with the HR Management System (HRMS)

Solution: all HRSSC employees with HRMS skills ratings lower than 4 out of 5 will take part in new HRMS courses that will be organised in-house by the system vendor. Also, one of the highest skilled employees will enroll into an expert course and will in the future act as an internal trainer/support person for other team members.

2   Equipment and applications

Since a lot of the problems affecting call duration are caused by equipment and applications failure, the team worked closely with the company's IT department to make a full assessment of the centre's hardware, software and network infrastructure and eventually find the solutions.

Problems: slow computers, HRMS hangs, slow network, computers go offline, and so on.

Solutions: in order to resolve these issues, a modernisation process was proposed that would contain the following steps:

- installing new computers for call centre operators (where possible upgrading old ones);

- changing the network access from wireless to cable to improve speed and uptime;

- changing the router to one with higher capacity that can cope with the high traffic needs of the HRSSC;

- upgrading the call centre switchboard.

Problem: for almost half of the received queries, there weren't any standardised procedures implemented in the HRMS workflow.

Solution: using the data collected during the measurement phase, the team was able to pinpoint those queries that were very often dealt with, but didn't have an automatic workflow implemented within the HRMS.

3   Methods

Problem: internal procedures are poorly documented and communicated.

Solution: a better organised internal communication process is to be put in place featuring:

- monthly team meetings focused on internal procedures (where the team can discuss, ask and give feedback about the internal procedures of the HRSSC);

- an online knowledge base was set up on the intranet that contains all internal procedures, well-documented and accessible either by key word searching or direct navigation.

CONTROL

Once the improvements are implemented and the new process is ready for hand off we need to make sure that these improvements will stand the test of time and the process will continue to perform in the way it was intended.

How many HR change projects do you know that have invested significant time and effort in creating change, only to find that a year later, things have slipped back to the old ways? The key to a change that lasts is effective control measures that extend beyond the life of the project, becoming part of the new operation.

Sample control phase steps

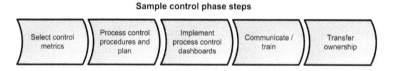

Figure 3.37   Sample control phase steps

The ongoing process control is usually the responsibility of one or more employees directly involved in the process, often the process owner. They may or may not be members of the *Six Sigma* team that conducted the project but must have the knowledge necessary to check the control metrics and act if needed. This may require some training during the implementation phase.

At this stage, a relevant set of control metrics should be selected by the *Six Sigma* team and operational teams, to be used to track that the process performance is within the desired limits. The most widely used control tools are control charts, run charts and process capability analyses. These tools can give early warnings if the process begins to go out of control or its capability decreases, so that corrective actions can be undertaken.

A continuous measurement process that can deliver the raw data to generate control reports will need to be implemented. For automated processes that are implemented as part of the organisation's core HR system, collecting this kind of data is just a question of implementing a few new features within the system. Standard HR systems such as SAP, PeopleSoft and Oracle will have the capabilities to capture and generate very useful reports in this area.

Process control metrics are often implemented as a dashboard report accessible through the self-service interface (ideally using the Internet browser), by the process owners or the employees who are in charge of monitoring the process.

Some key principles that *Six Sigma* teams should adhere to when defining control metrics and procedures are:

- control procedures must be simple, and easy to use;

- control metrics must be easy to understand;

- control metrics must have a real impact on the quality of the process;

- data collected must be unbiased;

- data collection and reporting must be automated as much as possible not to interfere with the day-to-day activities of the employees.

- metrics are chosen because they can:

    - detect early on when the process goes out of control,

    - detect early on when the capability of the process goes outside of the specification (service level agreements).

In order to communicate effectively a control and response plan must be developed and implemented. This plan will usually include:

- continuous measurement methods to be applied;

- control metrics and charts that will be checked;

- assigning roles and responsibilities to employees in charge of process control;

- actions to be taken in case the process goes out of control;

- scheduling control audit sessions in the medium term.

Transferring ownership of the process from the *Six Sigma* team to the operational team should be done after the new or improved process has been fully documented and the new process owners trained in controlling it.

Case study example – Part XI (Control)

C.1 Conclusions of the study

Two months after the implementation of the new improvements proposed by the *Six Sigma* team, the HRSSC experienced significant improvements in both customer satisfaction and cost reduction.

As seen in the 'before and after' comparison in Figure 3.38 opposite, the impact on call duration was extremely strong, not only reducing the average duration from 6 to 3.1 minutes but also making the process much more stable than before.

First call clearance also improved from 75 per cent to 91 per cent in less than 2 months after implementation.

Following these improvements, a new customer satisfaction survey showed a rating improvement from 3 to 4.3 which is very close to the best in class HRSSC.

C.2 Control metrics and future actions

To keep the new improvements under control, the team has chosen three of the most important metrics that will be monitored weekly. These metrics are:

- call duration (automatically monitored by the CRM solution);
- hand offs (implemented a new field in the centre's CRM solution in order to monitor all hand offs);
- average queue holding time (automatically monitored using data from the phone switch).

In order to monitor these metrics using control charts, a customised dashboard was configured to show X-bar control charts and highlight out-of-control symptoms automatically. Also, the contact centre supervisor was trained to monitor the quality dashboard and take the necessary actions.

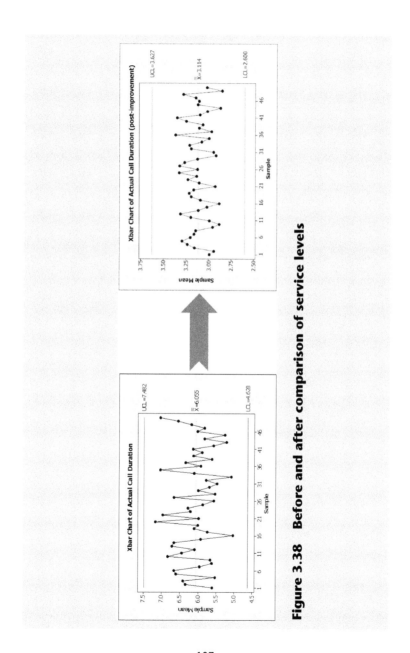

Figure 3.38   Before and after comparison of service levels

Lessons Learned from Delivering High Impact *Six Sigma* Projects

As we have illustrated, *Six Sigma* has great benefits for HR functions working to achieve excellence in service delivery. In this final chapter we review some lessons learnt along the way by *Six Sigma* experts, HR managers and consultants, through both *Six Sigma* and HR transformation projects.

1. CHOOSE THE RIGHT PEOPLE

Six Sigma projects demand a diverse set of scientific and softer skills, mindsets and personality types. Using this diversity ensures that the HR team will be able to manage the project and apply the rigorous statistical tools needed while at the same time generate innovative solutions and manage the people side of process improvement successfully. Look outside HR for statistical, technical and change management skills as well as to your HRBPs for your project team.

2. TRAIN, MENTOR AND INSPIRE THE TEAM

Committed employees, who believe in continuous improvement practices, have the necessary skills to apply them and are highly motivated, can deliver huge returns on investment by applying *Six Sigma* methods. To create such effective teams, a training programme on the methodology and tools of *Six Sigma* is usually not enough. Making sure that new *Six Sigma* belts are mentored by an expert such as a master black belt will increase the value their projects contribute to the organisation. Also, personal development strategies, coaching and Neuro Linguistic Programming (NLP) can contribute to improving the results that *Six Sigma* teams achieve.

3. LEVERAGE TECHNOLOGY

The complexity of quantitative analysis that *Six Sigma* projects need to deal with may sometimes seem overwhelming. But with the use of proper software tools, such as statistical packages or risk management applications, it is possible to perform even the most complex analyses or simulations, with minimal resources. In HR projects, besides using *Six Sigma* specific tools, teams must make sure that they can capture as much as possible of the needed information from the existing HRMS. Underutilisation of key HRMS features can often lead to gaps in performance specific data that can be valuable for process improvement projects. To make sure organisations get the most value out of technology during *Six Sigma* projects, an HRIT expert should be included in the team as a subject matter expert.

4. MEASURE WHAT NEEDS TO BE MEASURED

The Measurement phase is not a race to measure as much as possible. The quantity of the metrics used is nowhere near as relevant as their quality. It's better to focus on a few vital metrics and measure them well rather than measure everything.

5. TEST AND PROVE THE HYPOTHESES

Six Sigma is a scientific approach, keep this in mind throughout the project – the fact that it is a science based approach makes you focus on having testable hypotheses and empirical proof for your conclusions, a valuable tool for HR functions who are often labelled as not commercial.

6. BE AWARE OF POSSIBLE ERRORS

Don't rely completely on the conclusions that you see at first sight. In statistics there are Type I (Null hypothesis – 'seeing a difference when actually there is no difference') and Type II errors ('not seeing a difference when in reality there is'). What this means is that there is a probability that even if the numbers seem to prove one hypothesis to be true, it is actually false or vice versa. However this probability is usually small and in most cases it can be calculated.

7. SET SMART OBJECTIVES/REALISTIC SCOPE

SMART objectives (Specific, Measurable, Achievable, Realistic and Time-bound) help make your HR Transformation project more resource efficient and effective. Use these objectives for the project as a whole and for the team delivering it to maintain a clear way of managing project performance.

8. MANAGE CHANGE EFFECTIVELY

Each *Six Sigma* project brings changes to the organisation. Not managing the change in a proper way and not enabling the people involved in delivering the processes to accept and implement the changes well enough can destroy even a well-designed new or improved process that otherwise could have delivered most results.

Having the HR team adopt and follow 'new ways of doing things', from a new validation procedure to a whole replacement of the IT system, requires some sort of change management to be in place to make sure the improvements are able to generate the expected return on investment as soon as possible.

9. GET LEADERSHIP COMMITMENT

Leadership commitment to implementing *Six Sigma* in a consistent manner is essential to achieving results. Where organisation-wide *Six Sigma* initiatives are in place, Shared Services, including HR, will usually be included by default in these. However this doesn't mean that if the organisation doesn't have a high-level strategy for *Six Sigma* HR can not kick start its own initiative. A business case showing the feasibility of applying *Six Sigma* can back up HR's proposal and secure senior-level commitment.

(A1) Example Project Charter

Project Information	
Project Name	**Chartered Date**
HR SSC – Query process optimisation	01 March 2008
Sponsoring Organisation	**Project Start Date**
U Corporation	20 April 2008
Revision Number	**Target Completion Date**
1	01 September 2008

Team Sponsors	
Project Sponsor	**Contact Number**
Joe Doe	555-0001
Project Black Belt	**Contact Number**
George Edward	555-0002
Project Green Belt	**Contact Number**
Alice McGraw	555-0003

Additional Team Members		
Name	**Role**	**Contact Number**
Bruce Lee	Master Black Belt	555-0004
Name	**Role**	**Contact Number**
Thomas Edison	Technology Advisor	555-0004
Name	**Role**	**Contact Number**
Albert Einstein	Assessment Advisor	555-0004
Name	**Role**	**Contact Number**
Sun Tzu	IT support (2)	555-0004
Name	**Role**	**Contact Number**

Principal Stakeholders		
Name	**Role**	**Contact Number**
Harriet Brown	HR Manager	555-0023
Name	**Role**	**Contact Number**
Darren Buffet	CFO	555-0000
Name	**Role**	**Contact Number**
Gill Bates	CEO	555-0123
Name	**Role**	**Contact Number**

Project goals

1. Reduce time required to resolve customer phone queries to an average of 3 minutes.

2. Reduce the number of hand-offs by at least 20%.

3. Reduce call handling costs.

4. Increase first call clearance (one and done) rate.

5. Increase overall customer satisfaction.

Process problem

Since the opening of our Shared Services Centre 20 months ago, the time required to solve customer queries constantly increased from an average of 6 minutes per query to 8 minutes, while the number of total employees (who use the SSC's services) remained almost constant. This has in turn affected our customer satisfaction and total service costs to values that not only exceed our estimations but are also over 20% higher than the industry average.

Being an industrial services company, most of our employees don't have either the skills necessary to access the online self-service or available workstations from which they can access self-service channels. Therefore the most widely used contact channel of the HRSSC is the phone.

HRSSC Contact Channels

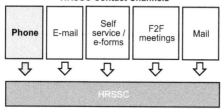

The team will present their findings and improvement proposals to the process owner at the end of July. Another report containing the control plan and results will be presented by the 1st of September.

Process importance

The high level "Query Management Process" of the HRSSC is of vital importance to our HR function and the organisation as a whole, as it manages and resolves most of the employee and line manager queries (>80%) for all HR areas such as:

- recruitment administration;

- pay and benefits administration;

- pensions administration;

- payroll administration;

- absence and leavers administration;

- employee data management;

- learning and development administration;

- fleet administration.

117

Authorised resources
<ul><li>1 desk for the black belt consultant within the SSC space;</li><li>meeting room available for the team as needed;</li><li>data access provided by the MI team to available metrics regarding the HRSSC operations;</li><li>budget to purchase benchmarking materials <£2,000;</li><li>access to the Galaxy data collection and assessment tools – customized by external consultants.</li></ul>

(A2) Software Packages Used for *Six Sigma* Projects

GENERAL *SIX SIGMA* SOFTWARE

Product	Developer	Features
Quality companion	Minitab Inc. www.minitab.com	"'Quality companion' from Minitab is one of the most comprehensive *Six Sigma* project management packages. The software contains tools for all stages of the *Six Sigma* methodology, including: • Tools (process mapping, fishbone, SIPOC, and so on) • Organisation tools (Gantt chart, dashboard, roadmap, project charter).

Product	Developer	Features
Sigma Flow	Compass Partners Inc.	Best practice *Six Sigma* project execution system. Features include: • Project selection • Project tracking and mentoring • Standards and best practice templates • Road maps • Project communications and metrics • Tools (value stream mapping, Fishbone, SIPOC).
SigmaSense	Grouputer	SigmaSense offers over 40 DMAIC tools presented in a structured way, to help *Six Sigma* belts and facilitators plan and implement process improvement projects. The software includes both statistical and business model type tools such as: • Run charts • Pareto analysis • Process sigma calculation • Force field analysis • Control plans • Process mapping • Surveys, and so on.

STATISTICAL/SIMULATION SOFTWARE

Product	Developer	Features
Minitab	Minitab Inc. www. minitab.com	Minitab is a statistical software package tailored for *Six Sigma* data analysis. It can perform all the statistical analyses needed for *Six Sigma* projects, such as: • Process capability calculation and plotting • Plotting histograms, bar charts, control charts, scatter plots, and so on. • Analysis of variance, and a lot more.
Statistica	Statsoft www.statsoft. com	Statistica (*Six Sigma*) is an analytic platform for planning, selecting and implementing *Six Sigma* projects. A scaleable solution that provides two categories: 1. Desktop – for single station use 2. Enterprise – multi-use collaborative The interface organises the tools needed according to the *Six Sigma* DMAIC methodology. The user can launch a *Six Sigma* toolbar with five submenus representing the five steps of DMAIC which contain tools needed by each stage. It is part of the Statistica suite of analysis software that provides an array of data analysis, data management, visualisation and data mining procedures.

Product	Developer	Features
@Risk **(Excel add-in)**	Palisade	@RISK is a Monte Carlo simulation software for Microsoft Excel capable of analysing thousands of different possible scenarios and computing their probability distribution. The tool can use multiple uncertain factors in computations, which can be defined using over 35 probability distribution functions or customised fitted probability distribution. It allows the user to set Upper and Lower Specification Limits and Target values and can perform a wide range of *Six Sigma* statistical and capability analyses such as Cpk, Cp, Cpm, and so on.
Stattools	Palisade	A complete suite of statistical analysis tools for Microsoft Excel. Stattools can perform a wide range of statistical analyses including: • Statistical inference (sample selection, hypothesis tests, ANOVA, and so on) • Nonparametric tests • Data management (categorical data, random sample generation, summary analyses and graphs) • Regression analyses (simple, stepwise) • Forecasting (moving averages, exponential smoothing) • Classification analysis • Normality tests • Regression analysis • Quality control (X-Bar, R, P, C, U, Pareto Charts).

PROCESS MAPPING/MANAGEMENT SOFTWARE

Product	Developer	Features
Nimbus Control 2007	Nimbus Partners	Nimbus Control 2007 provides a collaborative framework for mapping and measuring business processes, and for managing and improving them.
Smartdraw	Smartdraw.com	Business drawing software that provides templates and predefined libraries to draw flowcharts and almost any other diagrams needed in *Six Sigma* projects. Thousands of diagram elements/templates are available within libraries.
Visio	Microsoft	Microsoft Visio is a diagram building software that includes libraries for creating a wide range of diagram types such as: • Business diagrams • Process maps • Maps • Fishbone diagrams • And many others.
Flowcharter	iGrafix	iGrafx Flowcharter is a business process improvement software package that uses process analysis and modelling tools. The processes can be analysed using graphical representations that help present the information and focus on bottlenecks and issues in a process.

(A3) List of Useful Statistical Formulas

Below is a list of statistical formulas used in *Six Sigma* data analysis. Fortunately these formulas are already included as functions in different *Six Sigma* software packages.

Statistic	Excel formula	Mathematical formula
Range	=max(A1:A100) – min(A1:A100)	Maxvalue – minvalue
Population mean	=average(A1:A100)	$\mu = \dfrac{1}{N} \sum\limits_{i=1}^{N} x_i$
Variance	=var(A1:A100)	$\sigma^2 = \sum\limits_{i=1}^{N} \dfrac{(x_i - \mu)^2}{N} = \sum\limits_{i=1}^{N} \dfrac{\left(x_i - \dfrac{1}{N}\sum\limits_{i=1}^{N} x_i\right)^2}{N}$
Standard deviation	=stdev(A1:100)	$\sigma = \sqrt{\sigma^2} = \sqrt{\sum\limits_{i=1}^{N} \dfrac{(x_i - \mu)^2}{N}} = \sqrt{\sum\limits_{i=1}^{N} \dfrac{\left(x_i - \dfrac{1}{N}\sum\limits_{i=1}^{N} x_i\right)^2}{N}}$

Process capability formulas:		
Lower capability	n/a	$$C_{pl} = \frac{(\bar{\bar{x}} - LSL)}{3\sigma}$$
Upper capability	n/a	$$C_{pu} = \frac{(USL - \bar{\bar{x}})}{3\sigma}$$
Process capability index	n/a	$$C_p = \frac{USL - LSL}{6\sigma}$$

Further Reading

'*Transforming HR*' by Ian Hunter and Jane Saunders, Thorogood, 2005.

'The *Six Sigma* Handbook: The Complete Guide' by Thomas Pyzdek, McGraw Hill, 2003.

'*Six Sigma*: SPC and TQM in Manufacturing and Services' by Geoff Tenant, Gower, 2001.

'The Lean *Six Sigma* Pocket Toolbook: A Quick Reference Guide to 70 Tools for Improving Quality and Speed' by Michael L. George, John Maxey, David T. Rowlands and Malcolm Upton, McGraw Hill, 2005.

'Lean *Six Sigma* for Service: How to Use Lean Speed and *Six Sigma* Quality to Improve Services and Transactions' by Michael L. George, McGraw Hill, 2003.

'The *Six Sigma* Way: How GE, Motorola, and Other Top Companies are Honing Their Performance' by Peter S. Pande, Robert P. Neuman and Roland R. Cavanagh, McGraw Hill, 2000.

'The *Six Sigma* Black Belt Handbook (*Six Sigma* Operational Methods)' by Thomas McCarty, Lorraine Daniels, Michael Bremer and Praveen Gupta, McGraw Hill, 2005.

'The *Six Sigma* Project Planner: A Step-by-Step Guide to Leading a *Six Sigma* Project Through DMAIC' by Thomas Pyzdek, McGraw Hill, 2003.

GOWER HR TRANSFORMATION SERIES

This series of short books explores the key issues and challenges facing business leaders and HR professionals running their people management processes better. With these challenges comes the requirement of the HR function to transform, but the key question is to what and how?

The purpose of this series is to provide a blend of conceptual frameworks and practical advice based on real-life case studies. The authors have extensive experience in all elements of HR Transformation (having between them held roles as HR Directors and Senior Business Managers across a range of blue chip industries and been senior advisors in consultancies) and have consistently come up against the challenges of what is the ideal new HR model, what is the value of HR, what is the role of the HRBP and how can they be developed?

Whilst the guides all contain a mix of theories and conceptual models these are principally used to provide the books with solid frameworks. The books are pragmatic, hands-on guides that will assist readers in identifying what the business is required to do at each stage of the transformation process and what the likely options are that should be considered. The style is entertaining and real and will assist readers to think through both the role of the business and transformation project team members.

SERIES EDITOR

Ian Hunter is a founding partner of Orion Partners, a consultancy specialising in providing independent advice to organizations considering outsourcing their Human Resources department. He has worked for a number of leading management consultancies, including Accenture and AT Kearney and has been an HR Director in two blue chip organizations.

For Product Safety Concerns and Information please contact our EU
representative GPSR@taylorandfrancis.com
Taylor & Francis Verlag GmbH, Kaufingerstraße 24, 80331 München, Germany

* 9 7 8 0 5 6 6 0 9 1 6 4 3 *